China and the World

MW00748470

The emergence of China as a dominant regional power with global influence is a significant phenomenon in the twenty-first century. Its origin can be traced back to 1949 when the Chinese Communist Party under Mao Zedong came to power and vowed to transform China and the world. After the 'century of humiliation', China was in constant search of a new identity on the world stage. From alliance with the Soviet Union in the 1950s, China normalized relations with America in the 1970s and embraced the global economy and the international community from the 1980s. In *China and the World since 1945: An International History,* Chi-kwan Mark examines China's changing relations with the two superpowers, Asian neighbours, developing countries, and European powers.

The book offers an overview of China's involvement in the Korean War, the Sino-Soviet split, Sino-American rapprochement, the end of the Cold War, and globalization. It also assesses the roles of security, ideology, and domestic politics in Chinese foreign policy and provides a synthesis of the latest archival-based research on China's diplomatic history and Cold War international history. Examining the rise of China from a long-term historical perspective, it will be a valuable resource to students of Chinese history and contemporary international relations.

Chi-kwan Mark is Lecturer in International History at Royal Holloway College, University of London. His research interests focus on British–American–Chinese relations during the Cold War and Hong Kong's colonial and international history. He is the author of *Hong Kong and the Cold War: Anglo-American Relations, 1949–1957* (2004).

The Making of the Contemporary World
Edited by Eric J. Evans and Ruth Henig

The Making of the Contemporary World series provides challenging interpretations of contemporary issues and debates within strongly defined historical frameworks. The range of the series is global, with each volume drawing together material from a range of disciplines – including economics, politics and sociology. The books in this series present compact, indispensable introductions for students studying the modern world.

China and the World since 1945

An International History

Chi-kwan Mark

Routledge
Taylor & Francis Group

LONDON AND NEW YORK

First published 2012
by Routledge
2 Park Square, Milton Park, Abingdon, Oxon OX14 4RN

Simultaneously published in the USA and Canada
by Routledge
711 Third Avenue, New York, NY 10017

*Routledge is an imprint of the Taylor & Francis Group, an informa
business*

© 2012 Chi-kwan Mark

The right of Chi-kwan Mark to be identified as author of this work
has been asserted by him in accordance with sections 77 and 78 of
the Copyright, Designs and Patents Act 1988.

All rights reserved. No part of this book may be reprinted or
reproduced or utilised in any form or by any electronic, mechanical,
or other means, now known or hereafter invented, including
photocopying and recording, or in any information storage or
retrieval system, without permission in writing from the publishers.

Trademark notice: Product or corporate names may be trademarks
or registered trademarks, and are used only for identification and
explanation without intent to infringe.

British Library Cataloguing in Publication Data
A catalogue record for this book is available from the British
Library

Library of Congress Cataloging in Publication Data
Mark, Chi-Kwan.
China and the world since 1945: an international
history/Chi-kwan Mark.
p. cm. -- (The making of the contemporary world)
"Simultaneously published in the USA and Canada"--T.p. verso.
Includes bibliographical references.
China--Foreign relations--1949– 2. China–Foreign
relations--1912–1949. I. Title.
DS777.8.M37 2012
327.51--dc22
2011008295

ISBN: 978-0-415-60650-9 (hbk)
ISBN: 978-0-415-60651-6 (pbk)
ISBN: 978-0-203-80496-4 (ebk)

Typeset in Times New Roman
by Taylor & Francis Books

Printed and bound in Great Britain by the MPG Books Group

Contents

Preface

The emergence of the People's Republic of China (PRC) as a dominant regional power with global influence is a significant phenomenon in the twenty-first century. Its origin can be traced back to 1949 when the Chinese Communist Party (CCP) under Mao Zedong came to power and vowed to transform China and the world. This book is about the rise of China from the perspective of international history since 1945. It examines the aims, features, and ramifications of China's foreign policy and relations with the wider world. Viewing China's Cold War experiences as part of the long process of its full integration into the international community in the twenty-first century, the book links the past with the present and provides insight into the making of the contemporary world.

Looking at the 60 years from 1949 to 2009, one may be puzzled by the many twists and turns in China's foreign policy and international relations – from a revolutionary Communist state to America's 'tacit ally' to a responsible great power. Some scholars identify ideology as the main driving force behind Chinese foreign policy particularly during the Maoist period. Committed to the ideology of Marxism-Leninism, Mao Zedong and his comrades were determined to restore China's rightful position in the world. Others hold that *realpolitik* rather than ideology dictated China's foreign policy during the Cold War and especially in the age of reform since 1978. Like other sovereign states in the international system, China aimed to maximize its security, power, and wealth.

Ideology and security should not be seen in dichotomous terms, however. Thus, some scholars look beyond these two factors to explore the roles of perception, images, and identity in shaping Chinese foreign policy. Seeing international history as intercultural relations, they focus on how China viewed itself, defined its identity, and interacted with other powers in the world. At the heart of China's search for a new national identity after 1949 was the history and memory of the 'century of humiliation', a period when China became a victim of foreign imperialism.

This book, then, examines how China searched for power and security, class struggle and world revolution, and above all a new national identity on the world stage during the Cold War and beyond. Unlike most existing accounts of China's contemporary foreign policy and international relations, it takes a deliberately historical approach by devoting more space to the Maoist period (Chapters 1–7) than to the post-Mao reform decades (Chapters 8–10). Drawing upon the latest archival-based literature on China's diplomatic history and Cold War history, the book offers an updated overview of China's international history from 1949 to 1976. The chapters on the post-1976 period bring the story up to the twenty-first century, highlighting the continuity and change in China's foreign policy and international orientation.

This book is more a synthesis of the latest research findings of other scholars than an original, archival-based study. I, nonetheless, offer my own interpretation of major events within the framework of China's search for national identity after the 'century of humiliation'. Arranged chronologically and thematically, each chapter will look at China's interactions with the superpowers, Asian neighbours, Third World countries, and European powers, while engaging with the historiographical debate on the topic under study. In this volume, the pinyin system is used for the romanization of Chinese places and names (except Chiang Kai-shek, with which Western readers are more familiar). Due to space constraints, endnotes are kept to a minimum.

I wish to express my gratitude to Dr Alfred Lin, formerly of The University of Hong Kong, and Professor Rosemary Foot of Oxford University, both of whom inspired and guided my study of Chinese diplomatic/international history. I also thank Dr Eve Setch of Routledge, the anonymous reviewers of the original proposal and the manuscript, as well as the authors of the many books and articles on which my analysis was based. Any errors in this book are mine.

Chronology

1946–9		Chinese Civil War
1949	Oct.	PRC founded
	Dec.	Mao arrives in USSR
1950	Feb.	Sino-Soviet Treaty
	Oct.	China intervenes in Korean War
1951	May	'Peaceful liberation' of Tibet
1953	Mar.	Stalin dies
	July	Korean War Armistice
1954		Five Principles of Peaceful Coexistence formulated
	May–July	Geneva Conference on Indochina
	Sept.	First Taiwan Strait Crisis starts
1955	April	Bandung Conference
1956	Feb.	Khrushchev's 'de-Stalinization' speech
	Oct.	Polish and Hungarian uprisings
1957	Oct.	USSR launches Sputnik
1958		Great Leap Forward launched
	Aug.–Oct.	Second Taiwan Strait Crisis
1959		Three-year famine starts
	June	USSR cancels nuclear agreement with China

	July Aug.	Mao criticizes Peng Dehuai at Lushan Sino-Indian border clashes
1960		USSR withdraws experts from China
1962	Oct.	Sino-Indian Border War Cuban Missile Crisis
1963	Aug.	Partial Nuclear Test Ban Treaty
1963–4		Sino-Soviet open polemics Mao proclaims 'two intermediate zones'
1964	Jan. Oct.	France recognizes China China explodes atomic bomb
1964–5		US escalates war in Vietnam
1965	April	China–North Vietnam agreement on aid
1966		Cultural Revolution starts
1967		'Power seizure' in MFA
	Aug.	British Embassy in Beijing sacked
1968	Aug.	USSR invades Czechoslovakia
1969	Mar.–Aug.	Sino-Soviet Border War
1971	Mar.–April July Sept. Oct.	US table-tennis team in China Kissinger's secret visit to China Lin Biao killed in plane crash PRC admitted into UN
1972	Feb. Sept.	Nixon visits China; Shanghai Communiqué China and Japan establish diplomatic relations
1973	Jan.	Paris Agreement on Vietnam
1974	Feb.	Mao unveils Theory of Three Worlds

1976	Jan.	Zhou Enlai dies
	April	Tiananmen demonstration
	Sept.	Mao dies; Hua Guofeng becomes Party Chairman
1978	Dec.	Deng Xiaoping becomes paramount leader; Economic reform and opening-up policy adopted
1979	Jan.	China and America establish diplomatic relations
	Jan.–Feb.	Deng visits US
	Feb.–Mar.	China–Vietnam Border War
1982	Aug.	US–China Communiqué on US Arms Sales to Taiwan
	Sept.	'Independent Foreign Policy' proclaimed
1984	Dec.	Sino-British Joint Declaration on Hong Kong handover
1989	April–June	Tiananmen student protests end in military crackdown
	May	Gorbachev visits China
	June	Jiang Zemin becomes General Secretary
	End of 1989	Collapse of communism in Eastern Europe
1991	Dec.	Demise of USSR
1992	Jan.–Feb.	Deng Xiaoping tours southern China
1995–6		Crisis in the Taiwan Strait
1997	Feb.	Deng Xiaoping dies
	July	Hong Kong returns to China
	Oct.	Jiang Zemin visits US
1997–8		Asian financial crisis
1998	June	President Clinton visits China

1999	May	US accidental bombing of Chinese Embassy in Belgrade
2001	April	US spy plane collision
	July	Sino-Russian Treaty of Good-Neighbourliness; Shanghai Cooperation Organization founded
	Sept.	Terrorist attacks on US
	Dec.	China joins WTO
2002	Nov.	Hu Jintao becomes General Secretary
2003	Aug.	Six Party Talks on Korea
	Oct.	China–ASEAN Strategic Partnership
2004		Hu Jintao speaks of China's 'peaceful rise/ development'
2005	April	Anti-Japanese protests in China
2006		China–US strategic dialogues established
2008	Aug.	Beijing Olympics
2009	Oct.	Sixtieth anniversary of PRC

Abbreviations

ASEAN	Association of Southeast Asian Nations
ARF	ASEAN Regional Forum
CCRG	Central Cultural Revolution Group
CQ	*China Quarterly*
CCP	Chinese Communist Party
CPSU	Communist Party of the Soviet Union
CWH	Cold War History
CWIHPB	Cold War International History Project Bulletin
CWIHPWP	Cold War International History Project Working Paper
DH	Diplomatic History
GMD	Guomindang
EU	European Union
FRUS	Foreign Relations of the United States
GATT	General Agreement on Tariffs and Trade
IHR	*International History Review*
IS	International Security
JCWS	*Journal of Cold War Studies*
MFN	Most-Favoured-Nation
NPC	National People's Congress
PLA	People's Liberation Army
PRC	People's Republic of China
SARS	Severe Acute Respiratory Syndrome
SCO	Shanghai Cooperation Organization
UN	United Nations
WTO	World Trade Organization

Map

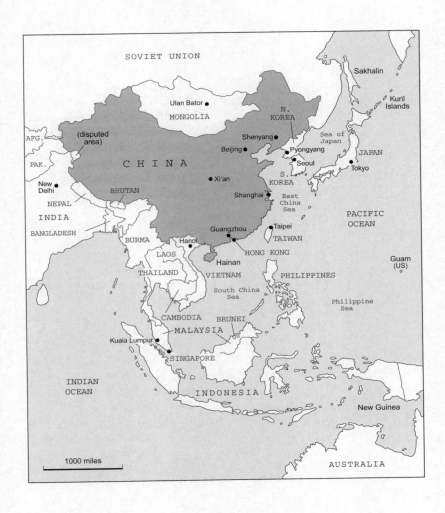

Introduction
History, ideology, and identity

As the founding leaders of the CCP, Mao Zedong (1893–1976), Zhou Enlai (1898–1976), and Deng Xiaoping (1904–97) were all born and brought up during the 'century of humiliation'. History and experience left a deep impact on them, shaping their characters, ideologies, and worldviews.

'Century of humiliation'

Until the late eighteenth century, China under the Qing dynasty had been a dominant force in East Asia. One of the world's oldest continuing civilizations, China or the 'Middle Kingdom' viewed itself as the centre of the universe. While not a completely isolated empire, Qing China was willing to engage with other civilizations or 'barbarians' only within the restrictive framework of the 'tribute system' and the Canton system. Foreign countries seeking diplomatic intercourse had to conform to the norms of Chinese ritual practice such as paying tribute and performing kowtow to the Chinese emperor, although the Qing court did demonstrate flexibility in treating China's closest neighbours and more distant states differently. Foreign traders eager to acquire Chinese goods such as silk and tea were confined to the city of Canton (Guangzhou) under strict business regulations.

The heyday of the Qing empire coincided with the rapid economic and military growth of Great Britain resulting from the Industrial Revolution. But while there was a huge demand for Chinese tea in Britain, a supposedly self-sufficient China was reluctant to purchase British industrial products in large quantities. In order to compensate for the unfavourable balance of trade, the British sold opium, produced in British East India Company-controlled India, to China. When, in 1839, the Qing court, worrying about the negative impact of opium-smoking, took forcible steps to stop the opium trade, the stage was set for the clash of the two empires – the First Anglo-Chinese War or, as the Chinese called it, the Opium War.

The First Opium War, which lasted until 1842, marked the onset of the 'century of humiliation' for China. Militarily defeated, China was forced to conclude 'unequal treaties' with Britain as well as other Western imperialist powers. According to the Treaty of Nanjing (Nanking), five Chinese cities were opened to foreign trade as treaty ports; Hong Kong was ceded in perpetuity to Great Britain; China was forced to pay indemnities; the rate of import tariffs was fixed; and foreigners were granted the right of extra-territoriality that exempted them from Chinese legal jurisdiction.

Owing to its desire to monopolize the opium market in China and to seek diplomatic residence in Beijing, Britain (joined by France) launched a second war against China between 1856 and 1860. Defeated and humiliated (notably by the looting and burning of the Old Summer Palace by the Anglo-French forces), China concluded a second round of 'unequal treaties' with the imperialist powers, opening more treaty ports and granting more diplomatic and economic privileges. In 1894–5, Japan joined the imperialist club by defeating and then imposing its 'unequal treaty' on China. This triggered a new phase of European imperialism in 1897–8 during which China was divided into spheres of economic and political influence by the Western powers. The year 1900 marked the climax of foreign humiliation of China: in response to the anti-foreign Boxer Rebellion, eight Western powers including Japan launched a joint expedition to Beijing, killing the Boxers, looting Chinese national treasures, and extracting heavy indemnities from a state that was on the brink of economic bankruptcy.

Foreign aggression together with serious domestic problems contributed to the collapse of the Qing dynasty in 1911. But the establishment of a Chinese Republic did not immediately end the suffering of China at the hands of foreign imperialism. In 1915, taking advantage of the European powers' preoccupation with the First World War, Japan put forward to Yuan Shikai's government the Twenty-one Demands, which, if accepted, would turn China into Japan's semi-colony. At the Versailles Peace Conference in 1919, Japan formally took over the former German rights in Shandong, thanks to the acquiescence of the Europeans.

During the Washington Conference of 1921–2, the United States, Japan, Britain, and other European powers endeavoured to create a stable 'post-imperial order' in the Asia-Pacific by restricting naval expansion, abrogating the Anglo-Japanese Alliance, and reconsidering their treaty rights in China such as customs control and extra-territoriality. Although, in the late 1920s, some minor concessions were made (for example,

Britain's return of Weihaiwei to China), the European powers were reluctant to give up their main privileges and interests in China. But the main threat to China's territorial integrity increasingly did not come from Europe. In 1931, Japan seized Manchuria in the Northeast; in 1937, it launched a full-scale attack on China, beginning what would be an eight-year-long war.

Yan'an leaders and quasi-diplomats

Against the background of domestic crises and foreign aggression, Mao, Zhou, and Deng began their revolutionary career that would bring them to power in 1949. For Mao, his early life was a long struggle for survival. Since its founding in 1921, the CCP was under the influence of the Moscow-led Communist International (Comintern) and the 'internationalists': Mao was a peripheral figure in the Chinese Communist movement. In unifying China in the 1920s, the Guomindang (GMD) or the Nationalist Party under Chiang Kai-shek (Jiang Jieshi) turned on the Communists, who on several occasions were on the brink of total destruction. To find a breathing space, Mao and his supporters undertook, from their southern base in Jiangxi Province, the Long March in 1934–5. Less than a tenth of them made it to remote Yan'an in Shaanxi in Northwest China. As a result of the epic Long March, together with Moscow's support, by 1936 Mao established himself as the paramount leader of the CCP. But his next struggle started as soon as his intra-party struggle ended.

On 7 July 1937, Japan exploited an incident at the Marco Polo railway bridge to launch a full-scale war against China. After the Xi'an Incident of December 1936, in which he was kidnapped by his generals so as to force him to fight the Japanese aggressors, Chiang agreed to form a second united front with the CCP against the common enemy. During the War of Resistance against Japan, Mao and his comrades conducted a strategy of guerrilla warfare behind the enemy lines and simultaneously developed their power base and forces in Yan'an and a number of border regions across the country.

During the war years, Mao formulated a quasi-official diplomacy of the CCP and developed a rudimentary foreign policy apparatus. Despite the united front with the GMD, Mao realized that the CCP needed allies from the outside world if the Communist revolution were to succeed. Ideology and survival instinct led him turn to the Soviet Union for material and moral support. During the Second World War, however, the Soviet Union put its global interests and the 'grand alliance' with the United States, Britain, and Nationalist China above the

CCP's cause. Nevertheless, Mao still maintained frequent and direct contact with Stalin (by radio and correspondence) and followed the Soviet leader's instructions. Although the relations between the CCP and the Soviets prior to 1945 were not always harmonious and smooth, they were still close and substantial.[1]

Besides, the CCP cultivated relations with the Americans within the framework of an international united front. Mao hoped to obtain US military aid against Japan and use Washington to restrain Chiang's power. The visit of American journalist Edgar Snow to the Communist-controlled bases in Shaanxi in mid-1936 was a breakthrough, representing Yan'an's 'first step toward joining the world'.[2] After spending four months in China and holding long interviews with Mao, Snow published what would be a widely circulated book titled *Red Star over China*, portraying the picture of a dynamic Chinese Communist movement. Thereafter, a dozen Western reporters visited the Communist bases, and helped disseminate a favourable image of the CCP.

In July 1944, the US Army sent an observers' mission, the so-called Dixie Mission, to Yan'an to establish quasi-official contact with the Chinese Communists and explore the possibility of intelligence and military cooperation in the war against Japan. In November, Patrick Hurley, President Franklin Roosevelt's personal envoy to Chiang, visited Yan'an to meet Mao and others in order to mediate in the growing conflict between the GMD and the CCP. Although the Dixie Mission did not result in a military alliance between Washington and Yan'an and the Hurley mediation, if anything, might have increased Mao's suspicion of America's motives, they represented the CCP's first official contacts with the United States.

To implement the CCP's foreign policy, a group of Long March veterans worked as a quasi-diplomatic mission. As early as November 1931, Wang Jiaxiang had been assigned as the 'People's Commissariat for Foreign Affairs' in the CCP-established 'Soviet Republic' in Jiangxi. By 1937, a 'Foreign Office' came into being in Yan'an, with Bo Gu as the 'Foreign Minister' and Wu Xiuquan as the Secretary-General. In 1939, under the instructions of the CCP Southern Bureau in Chongqing, a foreign affairs group was officially set up under the leadership of Zhou Enlai. A pragmatist and skilful negotiator, Zhou had long been involved in the external aspects of the Party's work, dealing with the Comintern, the GMD, and foreigners in China.[3]

After the founding of the PRC in 1949, the rudimentary foreign affairs institutions became part of the new Ministry of Foreign Affairs (MFA) headed by Zhou, who served as Premier and Foreign Minister (until early 1958). With their experiences in dealing with the Russians and the Americans and close working relations with Zhou, the Yan'an quasi-diplomats such as Wang and Wu formed the backbone of the MFA in its formative years.[4]

Zhou was more a policy implementer, however. Mao was the ultimate decision-maker on foreign policy. In the hostile Cold War environment, the policy-making process was highly centralized and personalized. As the paramount leader, Mao created an informal nuclear circle, consisting (at different times) of top CCP leaders such as Zhou, Liu Shaoqi (until 1966), Lin Biao (1966–71), and Deng Xiaoping (in 1975). Although the Politburo and its Standing Committee and the CCP Secretariat deliberated on important foreign affairs issues, Mao saw the meetings as venues to build consensus among his colleagues and to confer legitimacy on the decision that he favoured.[5]

Ideology and security

As a firm believer in Marxism-Leninism, Mao aspired to create a classless, egalitarian Chinese society free of feudalism, capitalism, and imperialism. Mao defined friends and enemies in terms of 'contradictions' – principal/antagonistic and secondary/non-antagonist – and applied the doctrine of 'united front' – tactical alignment with the 'middle-roaders' against the main enemy – to carry out class struggles. As a Communist theoretician, Mao 'sinicized' Marxism-Leninism by taking into account China's historical and geographical background. Realizing the weakness of the working class in a largely agrarian China, Mao emphasized the role of peasants in the revolutionary struggle against the GMD and the Japanese. And he applied it to foreign policy after 1949. Thus, he looked on the developing countries in Asia, Africa, and the Middle East as global 'peasants' – the 'countryside' – which would encircle and defeat the imperialistic capitalist world – the 'cities' – in the Cold War struggle.

For Mao, the Chinese revolution did not end in 1949 but needed to continue until all the imperialist influences and institutions on the mainland were destroyed, and China restored to its central position in the international system. Here lay his ideology of 'continuous revolution'.[6] To maintain the inner dynamics of revolution, Mao needed to constantly mobilize the Chinese people through domestic political campaigns and external crises. In this regard, there was a close connection between domestic politics and foreign policy in Mao's thinking. Furthermore, Mao was firmly committed to proletarian internationalism. Seeing the Chinese Communist revolution as part of the world proletarian revolution, he felt strongly that China had an obligation to promote revolutionary transformation abroad. To continue revolution at home and abroad after 1949 was essential to China's identity as a socialist state.

Mao and Zhou were also practitioners of *realpolitik*. Their main concern was to uphold China's national sovereignty and territorial integrity. Similar to other states in the international system, China's foreign policy was shaped by threat perceptions and security considerations. China needed to defend its long border, deter aggression, and fight wars if necessary.

Nevertheless, ideology and security (both state and regime) seemed to be two sides of the same coin. To promote continuous revolution at home and abroad was meant to ensure the survival of the PRC as a socialist state and to enhance the legitimacy of the CCP as the ruling party. In essence, Mao was a man of great complexities and contradictions: he was simultaneously idealistic and pragmatic, internationalist and nationalist.[7]

Search for national identity

China's foreign policy and international relations can be examined from the perspective of the search for national identity. A national identity 'enacts itself by assuming various national roles' and 'through interactions with other players in the same arena'.[8] It 'influences attitudes and policies alike, being the psychological foundation for the roles and behaviour patterns of a country in the international arena'.[9]

After 1949, how China defined itself, perceived its role in the world, and interacted with other powers were significantly shaped by the history and memory of the 'century of humiliation'. To eradicate the legacies of foreign imperialism was at the heart of China's search for a new national identity after liberation. But as Lowell Dittmer argues: 'Almost from the beginning, the PRC has been afflicted with a national identity dilemma.'[10] On the one hand, for the sake of ideological legitimacy and solidarity, China saw itself as part of the socialist bloc headed by the Soviet Union. On the other hand, as a newly independent and undeveloped nation, China identified with the oppressed peoples and nations in the 'Third World'. At times, the two identities coexisted easily. But at other times, nationalist aspirations came into conflict with proletarian internationalism, making it necessary for China to privilege one identity over the other. Nevertheless, there has been a consistent thread running through China's quest for national identity (or identities) on the world stage since 1949 – a strong desire to achieve national independence and equality after a century of foreign invasion and exploitation.

It is important to mention two ironies in China's search for a new national identity following the 'century of humiliation'. One was the salience of continuity across the divide of 1949. Essentially, the borders of the PRC corresponded to those of the Qing empire, which the Republic of China inherited. With the exception of Outer Mongolia, Communist China was in control of Manchuria (despite Soviet influence until the mid-1950s), Mongolia, and Tibet (which was 'peacefully liberated' in 1951). Besides, the Chinese Communists built on the success of the Nationalists in dismantling the treaty-port system in China. In the course of the 1930s, the Nationalist government regained control over tariffs, maritime customs, salt monopoly revenues, and nearly two-thirds of the foreign concessions in the treaty ports; in 1943 it concluded a treaty with Britain and the United States that formally abolished extra-territoriality and all foreign concessions. After 1949 Mao and his comrades continued the policy goals that the Republican leaders had set but failed to achieve – defending China against foreign aggression and seeking international recognition.[11]

Another irony was that, while repudiating the legacies of the 'century of humiliation', the CCP was keen to use the past to serve the present. During the Maoist era, the memory of 'national humiliation' was promoted to indoctrinate and mobilize the Chinese people against foreign enemies, notably the United States, which refused to recognize and respect New China. Despite proclaiming that the Chinese people had 'stood up', Mao could not rid himself of a 'victim mentality' after liberation. The post-Mao leaderships too invoked the 'victimization' discourse, especially after the Tiananmen crackdown in 1989 and the collapse of communism in Eastern Europe and the Soviet Union. The aim was not only to unite the Chinese nation in the light of the Western embargoes and the uncertain post-Cold War international environment, but also to shore up the declining legitimacy of Communist rule in the age of unprecedented economic reform.[12]

Notes

1 For studies emphasizing close CCP–Soviet relations prior to 1945, see Michael M. Sheng, *Battling Western Imperialism: Mao, Stalin, and the United States* (Princeton: Princeton University Press, 1997); Alexander V. Pantsov, 'How Stalin Helped Mao Zedong Become the Leader: New Archival Documents on Moscow's Role in the Rise of Mao', *Issues & Studies* 41: 3 (September 2005): 181–207.

2 Nui Jun, *From Yan'an to the World: The Origin and Development of Chinese Communist Foreign Policy* (1992), edited and translated by Steven I. Levine (Norwalk, Conn.: EastBridge, 2005), 21.

3 Lu Ning, *The Dynamics of Foreign Policy Decisionmaking in China* (Boulder: Westview Press, 1997), 40–2.
4 Xiaohong Liu, *Chinese Ambassadors: The Rise of Diplomatic Professionalism since 1949* (Hong Kong: Hong Kong University Press, 2001), 11–15.
5 Lu, op. cit., 8–11.
6 On this theme, see Chen Jian, *Mao's China and the Cold War* (Chapel Hill: The University of North Carolina Press, 2001).
7 See Michael H. Hunt, *The Genesis of Chinese Communist Foreign Policy* (New York: Columbia University Press, 1996).
8 Lowell Dittmer and Samuel S. Kim, 'In Search of a Theory of National Identity', in Lowell Dittmer and Samuel S. Kim (eds), *China's Quest for National Identity* (Ithaca: Cornell University Press, 1993), 15.
9 Robert A. Scalapino, 'China's Multiple Identities in East Asia: China as a Regional Force', in ibid., 215.
10 Lowell Dittmer, *Sino-Soviet Normalization and Its International Implications 1945–1990* (Seattle: University of Washington Press, 1992), 96.
11 On China's foreign relations and global connections during the Republican period, see William C. Kirby, 'The Internationalization of China: Foreign Relations at Home and Abroad in the Republican Era', *CQ* 150 (June 1997): 433–58; Frank Dikötter, *The Age of Openness: China before Mao* (Hong Kong: Hong Kong University Press, 2008).
12 On the memory and discourse of 'national humiliation' and its impact on China's foreign policy, especially in the post-1978 era, see Peter Hays Gries, *China's New Nationalism: Pride, Politics, and Diplomacy* (Berkeley: University of California Press, 2004); William A. Callahan, *China: The Pessoptimist Nation* (Oxford: Oxford University Press, 2010).

1   The Chinese Civil War and European Cold War, 1945–9

The Chinese Civil War of 1945–9 resulted in the establishment of the PRC and the transformation of East Asian international relations. While the conflict was domestic in origin, the outbreak of full-scale war in mid-1946 was significantly shaped by superpower politics. The final outcome was determined as much by the diplomacy of the two rival Chinese parties as by their military strategy and tactics. During 1949, Mao had to ponder on China's future relations with the Soviet Union and the United States, which remained in a state of constant flux.

Domestic causes

By the time Japan accepted unconditional surrender in August 1945, the GMD under Chiang Kai-shek remained in power in China. Yet in the course of the Sino-Japanese War, Chiang had lost some of his best armed units, and his government became increasingly corrupt and incompetent. If President Franklin Roosevelt had regarded Nationalist China as one of the 'Big Four' in the defeat of Japan and the construction of a post-war international order, his successor, Harry Truman, harboured serious reservations about the ability of Jiang to maintain stability and unity in China.

In the post-war years, the Nationalist government faced serious domestic problems. It alienated many of the urban elites (businessmen, intellectuals, and local leaders) by imposing new taxes, monopolies, and levies on them to finance the civil war. Economic mismanagement proved to have fatal consequences. To cope with escalating inflation, Nationalist officials relied on money printing, thus creating a vicious circle for the urban economy. By early 1949, the loss of legitimacy of the GMD state had reached crisis proportions. In January, Chiang announced his resignation from the presidency and his replacement by Li Zongren as 'acting president' (although Chiang remained the head of the GMD and was still influential in policy-making).

As a result of the Sino-Japanese War, the CCP became a viable political alternative to the GMD. The CCP transformed itself from a weak and disunited party into an efficient, highly disciplined, and mass-based organization, thanks to the leadership, charisma, and thinking of Mao. Through myth-making (such as the heroic myth of the Long March), theoretical writings (the 'Mao Zedong Thought'), and the rectification campaign of 1942–4 (in which Mao defeated his party rivals including Wang Ming), Mao established himself as the supreme leader of the CCP. Through moderate land reform and a de-emphasis on revolutionary ideology, Mao had attracted many peasants and other discontented elements to the Communist movement in the base areas.[1]

Nevertheless, by mid-1945 the balance of power between the GMD and the CCP was still very much in the former's favour. Militarily, the GMD forces were more numerous and better equipped, and controlled more territories, especially cities where the Communists were conspicuously absent. Diplomatically, Chiang's government was recognized by both the United States and the Soviet Union.

Cold War impact

During the final stage of the Second World War in early February 1945, the three Allied Powers' leaders, Franklin D. Roosevelt, Joseph Stalin, and Winston Churchill, met at Yalta to discuss war strategy and the post-war order. To secure a Soviet invasion of Japan, Roosevelt and Churchill agreed to Stalin's demands that the Soviet Union would establish a predominant position in Manchuria in Northeast China. The secret Yalta Agreement on China was confirmed in the Sino-Soviet Treaty of Friendship and Mutual Assistance, signed between the Nationalist and the Soviet governments on 14 August 1945, the same day as Japanese Emperor Hirohito announced unconditional surrender. Accordingly, the Soviets used Port Arthur (Lushun) as a naval base and exercised joint control over Manchurian Railways (the Chinese Changchun Railroad) for a period of 30 years. China accepted the independence of Outer Mongolia. The Soviet Union recognized the GMD as the legitimate government of China, and would withdraw its troops from Manchuria within three months after Japan's surrender.[2]

Stalin approached China from a global perspective. In establishing Soviet prominence in Manchuria, he had an eye on the security threat posed by Japan to the Soviet border. By recognizing the legitimacy of Chiang's government, Stalin aimed to continue the wartime collaboration with the United States and prevent the resumption of civil war in China. On the other hand, Stalin had few illusions about the strength of the CCP in a military showdown with the GMD. For these reasons, the Soviets prevented the CCP forces from entering the main cities and communication routes in the Northeast.

Although believing that the GMD forces were far stronger than the CCP's, Chiang realized that he needed a period of peace to resolve China's economic and other problems. With Washington's and Moscow's diplomatic recognition, Chiang was confident that he could exploit superpower politics to force the CCP into a subordinate political position and eventually destroy it. On the same day as Japan's surrender, Chiang invited Mao to Chongqing to discuss the political future of China. The Chongqing talks, from 28 August to 10 October, resulted in the Double Ten Agreement, which recognized the equality of all parties and called for the unification of military forces and the democratization of the central government.

Mao agreed to participate in the peace talks on Stalin's advice. Realizing that the CCP forces were no match for the GMD's and the prospect of substantial Soviet assistance was remote, Mao indeed had little room for manoeuvre. By following Stalin's instructions, Mao hoped that the Soviets would restrain Chiang from launching a full-scale attack on the CCP. In short, in August and September, the situation in China stabilized due to US–Soviet cooperation and Chiang's restraint.

But US–Soviet cooperation in China was fragile. Although the Truman administration aimed to prevent the outbreak of civil war, it also wanted to contain Soviet influence in Manchuria. Thus, from the outset, the US policy of 'neutrality' in the GMD–CCP struggle was compromised. In September, the United States landed more than 50,000 marines in Tianjin and other northern ports pending the arrival of Chiang's forces; it also airlifted and transported half a million GMD troops to take over strategic locations in the North and the Northeast. Moscow became increasingly suspicious of Washington's policy in China – and in Japan. At the Foreign Ministers' Conference between the United States, Britain, and the Soviet Union in mid-September, it became clear that the Americans wanted to exercise exclusive control over the occupation of Japan. To indicate their displeasure at US policies, in early October the Soviets encouraged the CCP troops to enter the Northeast and provided substantial Soviet weapons. But after Chiang launched, in November, a large-scale assault on the then Communist-controlled Shanhaiguan (which was the gateway to Manchuria), together with Washington's diplomatic pressure, Moscow backed down.

The United States did not want the situation to deteriorate further. In late November, General George C. Marshall was appointed as the President's special representative to China with the objectives of securing a ceasefire and a coalition government. As a result of the Marshall Mission, the two rival Chinese parties reached a ceasefire agreement in early January 1946, and a military reorganization agreement in late February. But when it came to implementation, Mao was unwilling to give up his independent armed force in creating a unified national army, for it would leave the CCP at the mercy of the GMD.

What finally ended the fragile peace in China was the emergence of the Cold War in Europe. By March, US–Soviet relations deteriorated rapidly over Eastern Europe. In consequence, Moscow announced the withdrawal of Soviet forces from Manchuria, which meant that the CCP was now allowed to occupy the main cities and transport routes in the Northeast. From April onwards, Mao sent CCP forces to replace the Soviet garrisons. By early May, the Soviets completed their withdrawal from Manchuria. In June/July, Chiang launched his large-scale assaults in Manchuria. The Chinese Civil War had erupted fully. Despite the fact that Marshall would stay on as mediator in China until early January 1947, it is clear that the United States could no longer exercise effective influence over the situation on the ground.

While planning his military campaigns, Mao, the Marxist theoretician, tried to clarify the relationship between the Chinese revolutionary movement and the growing US–Soviet conflict. One of the main issues to address was whether the Chinese Civil War would lead to a world war. In August, during an interview with visiting American journalist Anna Louise Strong, Mao talked of the concept of an 'intermediate zone'. To Mao, the 'main contradiction' in the world was that between 'the US reactionary clique' and the peoples of the 'intermediate zone' – capitalist, colonial, and semi-colonial countries of Europe, Asia, and Africa that separated the two superpowers. The United States would not unleash a third world war against the Soviet Union unless it controlled the 'intermediate zone'. As long as the peoples of the 'intermediate zone' persisted in their struggle against the American imperialists, Mao argued, a third world war could be avoided. As part of the 'intermediate zone', the CCP played an important role in the world-wide struggles of national liberation. Rather than causing a third world war, the Chinese Civil War thus contributed to world peace.[3]

Between mid-1946 and 1947, the Soviets provided more support to the CCP including weapons, military uniforms, and raw materials. Yet, the amount of aid was smaller than what Mao had expected and fell far below the level of US assistance to the GMD during this period. Although Marshall, who became Secretary of State upon his return from China in early 1947, ruled out direct US military intervention in China, the administration continued to provide military and economic aid to Chiang's government. As the Cold War in Europe gathered momentum in 1947, White House policy-makers and State Department officials had to mobilize support from Congress and the American public for the new grand strategy of containment. To secure congressional appropriations for the European Recovery Programme or the Marshall Plan, in 1947–8 the administration approved the China Aid Bill of 1948, which provided for $570 million worth of economic and military aid to the GMD government. In a word, the imperative of domestic mobilization for the European Cold War underscored the US involvement in the Chinese Civil War during 1947–8.[4]

US economic and military aid, however, was not enough to save Chiang's regime. From late 1947 onwards, the CCP forces began to seize the military initiative. In September Lin Biao launched an all-out offensive in Manchuria and basically conquered the entire region by November 1948. This decisive victory was followed by the capture of Beiping and Tianjin, the two major northern cities, and the battle of Huai-Hai, which involved more than a million men on each side fighting for the control of China north of the Yangzi River. By the end of January 1949, the Chinese Communists were in control of the northern half of China.

Establishing the principles of diplomacy

While planning his military operations south of the Yangzi, in early 1949 Mao contemplated the prospects for relations with the Soviet Union and the United States. Throughout the civil war, CCP–Soviet relations had been ambivalent and complicated, thanks to Stalin's global considerations and personal mistrust of Mao. In 1947 and 1948, Stalin had turned down Mao's requests for a visit to discuss Sino-Soviet cooperation. In 1948 Stalin fell out with Josip Tito, the leader of Yugoslavia, on the grounds of the latter's alleged deviations from Marxism-Leninism. Although the CCP quickly demonstrated its solidarity with Moscow, Stalin could not help but have doubts about Mao's credentials as a true Marxist, given the Chairman's emphasis on peasants rather than workers in the revolutionary struggle. It was feared that Mao would become a 'Chinese Tito' one day.[5]

Stalin's reservations about the CCP did not dissipate during 1949. In early January, Chiang, in his last-ditch attempt to prevent a total Communist victory, requested the Soviet Union to mediate the civil war. Historians have debated whether Stalin accordingly advised Mao not to cross the Yangzi River, but to seek a north–south division of China at the Yangzi. New research findings suggest that Stalin did consult with Mao about the prospect of a peaceful solution to the civil war through direct negotiation between the CCP and the GMD. His primary aim was to avoid a direct US–Soviet confrontation (especially at the time of the ongoing Berlin blockade), if not to keep the GMD in power. But when Mao indicated his strong objection to foreign interference in Chinese affairs, Stalin did not press the issue further.[6]

Mao, on the other hand, devised new principles and policies for dealing with the Western countries. Shortly after occupying Shenyang in Northeast China, in November 1948 the CCP's Military Control Commission in the city ordered all Western diplomats there to hand over their radio transmitters within 36 hours. The order was due partly to Moscow's advice and partly to the CCP's security concerns about American espionage activities in Shenyang. On Washington's instructions, the American Consul General in Shenyang, Angus Ward, refused to hand over the transmitter. On 20 November Ward was held under house-arrest by the PLA troops, and the consulate's offices and residential compound were confiscated. A year later, Ward and four of his colleagues were formally arrested on the grounds of espionage and finally expelled from China.

In handling the Ward case, Mao was simultaneously formulating the basic principles of New China's foreign policy, especially concerning diplomatic relations with the Western powers. Feeling strongly about the 'century of humiliation', Mao was determined to make a clean break with the old China. During the spring and summer of 1949, Mao developed the principles of 'making a fresh start' and 'cleaning the house before inviting the guests'. To Mao, the new Communist government would not recognize the legal status of any diplomatic establishments and personnel accredited to the former Nationalist regime as well as the treaties and agreements concluded or inherited by it. New China would establish diplomatic relations with all countries, including the Western ones, on the principle of 'equality'. But it would not be in a hurry to seek foreign recognition unless and until all vestiges of imperialist power and influence on the mainland were eliminated.[7]

In May/June the Chinese Communists established direct contact with American diplomats. After the fall of Nanjing in late April, on Washington's instructions, US Ambassador John Leighton Stuart was ordered to stay in order to protect American interests and remaining citizens in China and to maintain a channel of communication with the CCP authorities. A former missionary educator in China, Stuart felt that the United States could play a role in influencing the CCP's orientation and policy, for example, by offering US economic assistance to China after the civil war. Mao, for his part, wanted to explore the US attitude towards the CCP. In early May, Huang Hua, the director of the Bureau of Foreign Affairs in Nanjing, was asked to begin a series of secret talks with Stuart. (It was no coincidence that Huang was a graduate of Yenching University where Stuart had once served as president.) The talks touched upon the two governments' respective position and policy. In June, it was proposed that Stuart should visit Beiping to talk directly with Mao and other leaders.

In the summer of 1949, the Truman administration, preoccupied with European affairs, was pursuing an inconsistent and self-contradictory China policy. In view of the Communist occupation of Nanjing, in May the new Secretary of State, Dean Acheson, had laid down three basic conditions for US recognition of a new Chinese regime: the CCP's *de facto* control of territory, its willingness to discharge international obligations in full, and the general acquiescence of the Chinese people in its rule. The State Department ruled out the possibility of direct US intervention in China. But the Department of Defense was concerned about the impact of China's loss on Japan's security, while the Republicans in Congress and the China lobby warned against writing Chiang off. Consequently, Truman and Acheson decided on a strategy of continued military and economic assistance to the GMD to delay the inevitable for as long as possible. In other words, Acheson wanted to 'wait for the dust to settle': the United States would wait for the final collapse of the GMD and the emergence of a CCP government independent of Moscow before making the final decision on recognition.[8]

At the end of June, Truman vetoed Stuart's proposal for visiting Beiping. But this came as no great surprise to Mao, who used the Huang–Stuart talks mainly to explore Washington's real thinking and to prevent US intervention in China or subversion from within at the time of the Yangzi crossings. Now that both Nanjing and Shanghai had fallen into Communist hands, Mao concluded that New China would not establish diplomatic relations with any countries which maintained ties with the GMD. On 30 June, Mao proclaimed in a speech, 'On the People's Democratic Dictatorship', that China should 'lean to one side' in the bipolar Cold War, the side of the Soviet Union.

Mao's 'lean to one side' speech was meant to impress Stalin with his political loyalty and commitment to the socialist bloc headed by the Soviet Union. On 10 July, Liu Shaoqi, the Party's second in command, visited Moscow as a major step towards the formation of the Sino-Soviet alliance. Liu led a delegation comprising Wang Jiaxiang (a future ambassador to the Soviet Union) and Gao Gang (the Party head in Manchuria), both of whom were experienced in dealing with the Soviets. During their month-long stay, they held four formal meetings with Stalin and other Soviet leaders, covering important aspects of

Sino-Soviet relations. Recognizing that Mao now represented the true leader of China, Stalin apologized for his insufficient assistance to the CCP during the civil war. Liu sought Moscow's and Eastern European governments' diplomatic recognition of the soon-to-be-established People's Republic, which Stalin promised. Liu and Stalin agreed on a 'division of labour' in the promotion of world proletarian revolution: China, due to geographical proximity and similar historical background, would focus on the colonial and semi-colonial countries in the East, while the Soviet Union would concentrate on Europe. They also discussed Sino-Soviet military cooperation. As a result of Liu's visit, the Soviets promised to help China to establish an air force, dispatch a team of Soviet experts to assist China's economic reconstruction and military build-up, and offer loans of $300 million.[9]

If a strategic Sino-Soviet alliance was in the making, by the summer of 1949 Mao's hostility towards the United States reached new heights, not least due to Washington's tacit support for the Nationalist blockade of China's eastern coast following Shanghai's fall. But the decisive battles of the civil war were all but over. Chiang retreated to Taiwan, bringing with him American weapons, gold reserves, and art treasures. The United States wanted to draw a political line with the failed GMD state on the mainland. In August, the State Department published the *China White Paper*, a huge volume of documents and analyses on pre-1949 US–China relations. In his open letter of transmittal of 30 July, Secretary Acheson defended the administration's opposition to full-scale intervention in the civil war, attributed the GMD's defeat to its misuse of US aid and its own inefficiency, and expressed the American hope that Chinese nationalism would eventually reassert itself against Soviet domination.[10] Unconvinced, Mao responded to the *China White Paper* by launching a nationwide anti-American propaganda campaign. In August the Xinhua News Agency published four consecutive articles written by Mao. In the article which appeared on 28 August, Mao denounced the White Paper as 'a counter-revolutionary document which openly demonstrates US imperialist intervention in China'.[11] Mao wanted to mobilize the Chinese people behind his anti-American policy.

On 1 October, Mao proclaimed on top of Tiananmen, or the Gate of Heavenly Peace, that the Chinese people had 'stood up'. Mao's China had formally joined the world.

Lost chance or no chance?

Was there a 'lost chance' for Sino-American accommodation in 1949? By using American documents and looking primarily from the American perspective, Warren Cohen and Nancy Tucker have put forward a 'lost chance' thesis on the basis of the troublesome CCP–Soviet relationship during the civil war, the Huang–Stuart talks, as well as the Department of State's 'hands-off' approach towards Taiwan. Given Stalin's reservations about the CCP on the one hand, Acheson's frustration with the GMD regime on the other, they argue, the Chinese Communist leadership was indeed flexible enough to reach a certain degree of accommodation with the United States, such as limited economic and political contact, if not full diplomatic recognition. But the Truman administration, under the influence of domestic and Cold War politics, was too inflexible to respond positively to the opportunities provided by, for example, Stuart's proposed visit to Beiping. The United States thus helped push Mao and the CCP to the side of the Soviet camp, thereby missing a 'chance' for Sino-American accommodation.[12]

By using Chinese archival sources, Chen Jian and Thomas Christensen found no evidence for any 'chance', highlighting instead the closeness of Sino-Soviet relations and the informal and exploratory nature of the Huang–Stuart contacts. Chen argues that Mao was determined to transform the Chinese state and society and to restore China's rightful position in the international system. For all the difficult moments in CCP–Soviet relations, Mao realized that Stalin's support was vital to the defeat of the Nationalists as well as his 'continuous revolution' after nationwide liberation. The Ward case reflected Mao's growing hostility towards the Americans, while hardening the Truman administration's attitude towards recognition of the CCP. Mao did not regard the informal Huang–Stuart talks as serious bridge-building for Sino-American accommodation. In 1949 he was not in a hurry to seek US recognition, given Washington's reluctance to cut all links with the GMD. The 'lost chance' thesis is therefore more myth than reality. Looking from the Chinese perspective and using Chinese archival sources, Chen and Christensen have avoided an America-centric approach that treated Mao or the CCP as a passive actor in the US–China relationship: China was not for the United States to 'gain' or 'lose'.[13]

In sum, in October 1949, Mao was in little doubt that China's new identity was to be a loyal ally of the socialist bloc headed by the Soviet Union.

Notes

1 See Suzanne Pepper, *Civil War in China: The Political Struggle, 1945–1949* (Berkeley: University of California Press, 1978); Odd Arne Westad, *Decisive Encounters: The Chinese Civil War, 1946–1950* (Stanford: Stanford University Press, 2003), 2–13.

2 My interpretation draws heavily on Odd Arne Westad, *Cold War and Revolution: Soviet–American Rivalry and the Origins of the Chinese Civil War, 1944–1946* (New York: Columbia University Press, 1993); Chen Jian, *Mao's China and the Cold War* (Chapel Hill: The University of North Carolina Press, 2001), 26–37.

3 Niu Jun, *From Yan'an to the World: The Origin and Development of Chinese Communist Foreign Policy* (1992), edited and translated by Steven I. Levine (Norwalk, Conn.: EastBridge, 2005), 288–9.

4 On this theme, see Thomas J. Christensen, *Useful Adversaries: Grand Strategy, Domestic Mobilization, and Sino-American Conflict, 1947–1958* (Princeton: Princeton University Press, 1996), 32–76.

5 On CCP–Soviet relations during the Chinese Civil War, see Niu Jun, 'The Origins of the Sino-Soviet Alliance', in Odd Arne Westad (ed.), *Brothers in Arms: The Rise and Fall of the Sino-Soviet Alliance, 1945–1963* (Stanford: Stanford University Press, 1998), 57–64.

6 Ibid., 64–5; Westad, *Decisive Encounters*, 216–19.

7 Chen Jian, *China's Road to the Korean War: The Making of the Sino-American Confrontation* (New York: Columbia University Press, 1994), 33–44.

8 See Nancy B. Tucker, *Patterns in the Dust: Chinese–American Relations and the Recognition Controversy, 1949–1950* (New York: Columbia University Press, 1983).

9 Chen, *China's Road to the Korean War*, 71–7; Sergei N. Goncharov, John W. Lewis, and Xue Litai, *Uncertain Partners: Stalin, Mao, and the Korean War* (Stanford: Stanford University Press, 1993), 61–75.

10 *The China White Paper, August 1949* (Stanford: Stanford University Press, 1967), iii–xvii.

11 *Selected Works of Mao Zedong*, vol. iv (Beijing: Foreign Language Press, 1969), 441–5.

12 Warren Cohen, 'Introduction' to 'Symposium: Rethinking the Lost Chance in China', *DH* 21 (Winter 1997): 71–5; Tucker, op. cit.

13 Chen Jian, 'The Myth of America's "Lost Chance" in China: A Chinese Perspective in Light of New Evidence', *DH* 21 (Winter 1997): 77–86; Thomas J. Christensen, 'A "Lost Chance" for What? Rethinking the Origins of US–PRC Confrontation', *Journal of American–East Asian Relations* (Fall 1995): 249–78.

2 The Sino-Soviet Alliance and the Korean War, 1950–3

After 1 October 1949, the PRC took immediate steps to establish diplomatic relations with other socialist countries, and formed a politico-military-economic alliance with the Soviet Union. It strove to complete the task of national unification. Between 1950 and 1953, China was involved in the Korean War for ideological and security reasons. Mao defined China's identity as a close ally of the Soviet socialist bloc and an independent sovereign state.

Diplomatic relations with the Soviet bloc

At the inauguration ceremony of the PRC on 1 October, Mao Zedong proclaimed that the Central People's Government was 'prepared to establish diplomatic relations with any foreign government which is willing to observe the principles of equality, mutual benefit, and mutual respect of territorial integrity and sovereignty'.[1] For ideological reasons, China gave priority to the Soviet Union and East European countries: no negotiations were required to establish diplomatic relations. The Soviet Union was the first country to recognize the PRC. On 2 October, the Soviet Vice-Foreign Minister, Andrei Gromyko, sent an official note to Chinese Foreign Minister Zhou Enlai, and simultaneously took the step to sever relations with the GMD government, then officially located in Guangzhou, by withdrawing the Soviet diplomatic envoy from the city. In his reply the next day, Zhou agreed to the prompt establishment of diplomatic relations. The 'people's democracies' in Eastern Europe quickly followed suit. Between 4 October and 23 November, China established diplomatic relations with all Eastern European countries except Yugoslavia, together with the Democratic People's Republic of Korea on 6 October and the Socialist Republic of Vietnam on 18 January 1950.[2]

But Mao needed more than Moscow's diplomatic recognition. The Chairman was determined to replace the 1945 Sino-Soviet Treaty between the GMD and the Soviets by a new treaty. Only by abolishing this 'unequal treaty', Mao believed, could New China really make a clean break with the past and set a good precedent for abolishing similar treaties with the Western capitalist countries. For that purpose, Mao renewed his request for a visit to Moscow, which Stalin could hardly rebuff this time round. On 16 December, Mao for the first time set foot on Soviet soil, together with a small group of personal aides.[3]

At six o'clock that evening, Mao held his first meeting with Stalin and other Kremlin leaders. It turned out to be an unpleasant and unproductive encounter. Mao was partly responsible for the uneasy atmosphere: he was deliberately ambiguous about the main objective of his trip. Stalin, for his part, made no personal apology for the Soviet mistakes during the Chinese revolution, an apology which Mao had expected. (Although Stalin had apologized during Liu Shaoqi's visit in July/August, to repeat it to the Chinese paramount leader was quite a different matter.) Besides, Stalin wanted to preserve the 1945 Treaty, which established the Soviet sphere of influence in Manchuria on the basis of the Yalta understandings with the United States.

Further talks between Stalin and Mao went nowhere. By early January 1950, Mao could not but reveal to his comrades in Beijing the bad treatment that he had received in Moscow. (In the Western press, there were even rumours that Mao was under house arrest.) To exert pressure on Stalin, on 2 January Mao disclosed in an interview with a Tass correspondent that the 'existing' Sino-Soviet Treaty was the key question that had to be settled, thus indicating his desire for a new treaty. Later, Stalin agreed with Mao that Zhou Enlai would come to Moscow to negotiate the details of a new Sino-Soviet treaty.

On 20 January, the arrival of Zhou with a large Chinese delegation kick-started the negotiation. By 9 February, Mao, Zhou, and Stalin basically agreed on the terms in all the documents constituting the main treaty and additional agreements. Signed on 14 February, the Sino-Soviet Treaty of Friendship, Alliance and Mutual Assistance, which remained in force for a term of 30 years, stipulated that China and the Soviet Union would render military and other assistance to each other should Japan or states allied with it attack either of the two Contracting Parties. Separate agreements guaranteed that the Soviet Union would give up its privileges in the Chinese Changchun Railroad and in Lushun by the end of 1952. The Soviets would grant a loan of $300 million at 1 per cent annual interest and send technicians to assist China's economic reconstruction. China in turn recognized the independence of Outer Mongolia.[4]

To Stalin, the alliance with China strengthened the Soviet strategic position in the Cold War with the United States. Besides, Stalin hoped to avert a possible rapprochement between China and the West. On 5 January, President Truman had given a speech on his 'hands-off' policy towards Taiwan, according to which the United States would not intervene militarily in the Taiwan Strait nor provide further military aid to Chiang's regime. The following day, Britain announced its diplomatic recognition of the PRC. When bargaining with Mao and Zhou over a new treaty around that time, Stalin certainly had the bigger strategic picture in mind.[5] As for Mao, the massive economic and military aid provided by the Soviets was vital to the construction and strengthening of New China. True, Mao might have felt that he had been badly treated by the arrogant Stalin in Moscow, but any ill-feeling and bitterness towards the Soviet leader were suppressed by the Chairman for the sake of proletarian internationalism.

Negotiations before diplomatic relations with capitalist countries

China adopted a different approach to developing relations with capitalist countries. It insisted on negotiations before the establishment of diplomatic relations. Non-socialist countries were required to send representatives to Beijing for negotiation, especially in clarifying their attitudes towards the 'GMD clique'. Only by demonstrating their 'sincerity' and taking concrete steps to sever all links with Jiang's regime would China agree to establish diplomatic relations.

Burma was the first non-socialist country to accord diplomatic recognition to the PRC. But on 1 April, India became the first non-socialist state to establish diplomatic relations with China due to the earlier arrival of the Indian negotiating representative in Beijing, and China's satisfaction with the Indian attitude and policy towards the GMD. Between 1950 and early 1951, Burma, Pakistan, Sweden, Denmark, and Switzerland all managed to establish diplomatic relations with China after fairly smooth negotiations.[6]

Britain was also one of the first Western countries to recognize the People's Republic – on 6 January 1950. The Labour government aimed to preserve British economic interests on the mainland, retain Hong Kong, and drive a wedge into the Sino-Soviet alliance through positive engagement with China. But Sino-British negotiations over diplomatic relations, which began in early March, turned out to be protracted and complicated, thanks to the British legal position on Taiwan and the Anglo-American 'special relationship'.

During the negotiations, the Chinese side asked the British representative to clarify two issues. One concerned the British policy on voting regarding Chinese representation in the United States. In January, Britain had abstained from voting on a Soviet resolution to expel the GMD representative from the UN in order to maintain solidarity with America. The other had to do with the British attitude towards GMD organizations and China's state properties in Hong Kong. In late 1949, two aviation companies – one pro-American/Chiang, the other Beijing-owned – were involved in a legal dispute over the ownership of 71 aircraft grounded in Hong Kong. Although, in February 1950, the Hong Kong court ruled that the aeroplanes belonged to the PRC, London was under pressure from Washington to prevent them from falling into Communist hands. Not satisfied with the British ambivalent attitude towards the GMD, Beijing thus refused to reciprocate London's diplomatic recognition. Sino-British negotiation ended abruptly when the Korean War broke out in the summer of 1950.[7]

National unification with Hong Kong, Tibet, and Taiwan

In late 1949 and 1950, China sought to complete the task of national unification. While being firm on the principle of national sovereignty and territorial integrity, Mao was rather flexible in his approach towards recovering lost/disputed territories. Three cases deserve examination here – Hong Kong, Tibet, and Taiwan. China demonstrated considerable flexibility as to the specific steps for recovering Hong Kong. Regarding Tibet, China was flexible enough to use a combination of military and political means, and to distinguish between short-term and long-term goals. Beijing's attitude towards unification with Taiwan was most uncompromising.

During 1949, Mao made the decision to leave British Hong Kong alone. Hong Kong, comprising Hong Kong Island, Kowloon Peninsula, and the New Territories (including some two hundred islands), had been annexed or leased by Britain under the Treaty of Nanjing (1842) and the two Treaties of Beijing (1860 and 1898). To the Chinese leaders, the three treaties were 'unequal' and thus 'illegal' and 'invalid'. As an inalienable part of China, they claimed, Hong Kong was merely under British 'administration'.

Nevertheless, to Premier Zhou Enlai, China's Hong Kong policy should not be dictated by 'the narrow principle of territorial sovereignty' but should be seen as 'part of the strategic arrangements for the general East–West struggle'. As the Cold War intensified in Asia, Hong Kong served as an outpost for gathering intelligence on the outside world, a valuable port to obtain prohibited goods and capital, as well as a wedge to split the Anglo-American alliance. To the CCP leaders, Hong Kong was a problem 'left behind by history', and its resolution would be 'a long-term task'. Although it was not one of their immediate priorities, they realized that the 99-year lease of the New Territories would expire in 1997. Mao defined the guiding principles of China's Hong Kong policy as 'long-term planning and full utilization'.[8]

While delaying Hong Kong's retrocession, Mao was determined to assert China's sovereignty over Tibet in 1949–50. A historic buffer zone among the competing regional powers and a *de facto* independent Lamaist state in the first half of the twentieth century, Tibet was deemed an integral part of China. To Mao, China was a multinational country built on the notion of 'a republic based on the unity of five nationalities' consisting of Hans, Manchus, Mongolians, Hui Muslims, and Tibetans. He proudly believed in the liberation of the semi-feudal and 'backward' theocratic state.[9]

Initially, China had relied mainly (but not exclusively) on military means to liberate Tibet, and expected to complete the occupation of Chamdo, where the main force of the Tibet army was stationed, by the spring of 1950. But due to logistical problems, it placed a greater emphasis on unification through negotiation, while continuing military preparations. Since early 1950, the Chinese government repeatedly called for the government of Tibet to dispatch representatives to Beijing for negotiations over the 'peaceful liberation' of Tibet. To force the Tibet elites to the negotiating table, China launched a military campaign in Chamdo on 6 October, achieving a decisive victory two weeks later. There followed not a military invasion of Central Tibet, but an intensified campaign for 'peaceful liberation'.[10] In an open statement on 10 November, Beijing emphasized that in return for Lhasa's acceptance of Tibet as an integral part of China, Tibet's feudal and theocratic system would be preserved, and the Dalai Lama's status unchanged.

During 1950, Lhasa appealed to the international community to oppose China's intrusion, but to no avail. In late January 1951, the Dalai Lama expressed his willingness to negotiate with the Chinese government. On 29 April, Tibetan representatives from Lhasa arrived in Beijing to begin negotiations. On 23 May, the Seventeen-Point Agreement for the Peaceful Liberation of Tibet was signed, according to which Beijing agreed (for the time being) to maintain Tibet's political, economic, and social systems while Lhasa acknowledged China's sovereignty over Tibet. The 'peaceful liberation' of Tibet strengthened the credibility and legitimacy of China's sovereignty claims, or so Mao believed.

Like Tibet, Mao was determined to achieve unification with Taiwan in the early years of the PRC, but he pursued it primarily by military means. Following its surrender in August 1945, Japan had returned Taiwan (together with other 'stolen' territories such as Manchuria) to China on the basis of the 1943 Cairo Declaration between America, Britain, and Nationalist China and the subsequent Potsdam Declaration of 1945 that confirmed it. But with the onset of the Cold War in the late 1940s, the United States and Britain contended that Japan had only renounced its claim over Taiwan but had yet to return the island to China pending the conclusion of a peace treaty. What complicated the status of Taiwan was the existence of the 'two Chinas' after 1949: both the CCP and the GMD each claimed to be the only legitimate government of China.

Nonetheless, Mao would have none of the legal arguments about China's sovereignty over Taiwan. In the light of Truman's January speech on the US 'hands-off' approach towards the island, Mao and his military generals expected to liberate Taiwan in the summer of 1950. They planned to start with assaults on Hainan and other off-shore islands such as Zhoushan and Jinmen before capturing Taiwan. But by early June, the difficulties of amphibious operations as revealed in the failed Jinmen campaign (China had inadequate naval units and almost no air force), together with the hardening of the US attitude towards Communist expansion, forced Mao to postpone an attack on Taiwan until the spring or summer of 1951. But the outbreak of the Korean War completely shattered Mao's unification plan.[11]

The Korean War and Chinese intervention

On 25 June, Communist North Korea under Kim Il-sung invaded pro-Western South Korea led by Syngman Rhee. The idea of an invasion was Kim's, but from the outset, his calculations and planning could not be separated from the international politics of the great powers. As early as March 1949, Kim had raised with Stalin the question of Soviet support for an invasion, only to be rebuffed by the Soviet leader. During Kim's three-week visit to Moscow in late March/early April 1950, Stalin gave the green light for the North Korean invasion plan which, Kim claimed, would involve a short war without triggering US intervention. Stalin supported it because of the Soviet acquisition of atomic bombs, the formation of the Sino-Soviet alliance, and America's exclusion of South Korea from its 'defence perimeter' in the Pacific. Nevertheless, determined to avoid a direct confrontation with the United States, Stalin insisted that the Soviet Union would not directly participate in the fighting, and instead asked Kim to consult with Mao about the use of Chinese troops if necessary.[12] By involving China in a war over Korea, the paranoid and calculating Stalin wanted to destroy once and for all the chance of accommodation between China and the Anglo-American camp.[13]

During Kim's visit to Beijing in mid-May, Mao gave his approval to a North Korean invasion. Preoccupied with his own invasion of Taiwan by that time, Mao could hardly decline Kim's request for assistance without jeopardizing Stalin's support for China. Ideologically, Mao was eager to seize the opportunity provided by the Korean War to maintain the dynamics of his 'continuous revolution'. By involving the Chinese population in a mass mobilization campaign under the banner of 'Resist America and Assist Korea', Mao hoped to speed up the transformation of the Chinese state, society, and economy. Furthermore, the North Korean Communists had been important allies of the CCP, fighting shoulder to shoulder with their Chinese counterparts during the Sino-Japanese War and the Chinese Civil War. Proletarian internationalism meant that Mao had to repay the Chinese debt to his fellow North Korean comrades. Although believing US intervention to be unlikely, Mao firmly asked Kim not to exclude this possibility and enquired whether the dispatch of Chinese troops to the Sino-Korean border was required in the event of American involvement. Kim insisted that the war would be finished within a month before Washington would be able to respond.[14]

To the three Communist allies' surprise, the United States responded swiftly and decisively to the North Korean attack, organizing a United Nations (UN) coalition force to repel the aggressors from South Korea. More importantly for China, Truman ordered the dispatch of the US Seventh Fleet to 'neutralize' the Taiwan Strait. To the President, the aim was to prevent a possible escalation of hostilities beyond the Korean peninsula by separating the two rival Chinese states. To Mao, however, the decision was a reversal of Washington's 'hands-off' approach towards Taiwan in order to perpetuate the division of China.

On 15 September, the American-led UN coalition force headed by General Douglas MacArthur landed at Inchon. The large-scale counter-attack successfully forced the invading North Korean troops out of South Korea. Having achieved the original war aim of liberating South Korea, the Truman administration decided to roll back communism in Asia. On 7 October, the American First Cavalry Division crossed the thirty-eighth parallel that separated the two Korean states, and the North Koreans, unaided, were forced to retreat northward. A week later, the American forces advanced towards the Chinese–Korean border at the Yalu River.

Despite Mao's promise, China had not started military preparations prior to the North Korean assault. In the first week of July, Stalin began to encourage Mao to prepare for China's entry to the Korean War. Beijing established the Northeast Border Defence Army for military actions in North Korea if necessary. After the successful US landing at Inchon, a desperate Kim requested Stalin to urge Mao to provide military support for Pyongyang. On 1 October, Stalin sent a carefully worded message to Mao and Zhou, asking them to provide the promised assistance to Kim.

In response to the deteriorating situation in Korea, Mao personally drafted a message to Stalin, dated 2 October, stating that China would send troops to the peninsula shortly. But what Stalin received from Mao was a completely different message, which said that Beijing needed to reconsider the desirability of military intervention. Declassified Chinese and Russian documents show that Mao had written but not sent the original message on the dispatch of Chinese troops (thus explaining why this message could be found only in the Chinese Central Archives but not in the Russian documentation). In his actual reply to Stalin (which was conveyed in a 3 October telegram to Stalin by the Soviet Ambassador to China), Mao listed a number of reasons behind his reservations about China's intervention: that the Chinese troops were 'extremely poorly equipped'; that Beijing's entry into the Korean War would 'provoke an open conflict between the USA and China'; and that his government's 'entire plan for peaceful construction [would] be completely ruined'.[15] The real reasons, though, were divided opinions within the CCP leadership and Mao's desire to bargain with Stalin about Soviet air support.[16]

Although Mao was ideologically committed to Kim's revolutionary cause, he could not completely ignore the concerns of other CCP leaders who saw domestic economic reconstruction as a higher priority than the Korean War. Mao was eager to persuade his colleagues to accept his views. Besides, Mao felt that China needed Soviet air support in view of the technologically superior American forces. But in his 1 October letter to Mao, Stalin had not committed himself to the provision of Soviet air cover for the Chinese troops in Korea.

On 3 October, Zhou Enlai asked Indian Ambassador K. M. Panikkar to warn Washington that China would intervene in Korea should the United States cross the thirty-eighth parallel. The warning was, however, ignored by America. On 7 October, the US/UN forces began to fight their way into North Korea. The next day, Mao issued the order to organize the Chinese People's Volunteers to assist the Korean people's war of liberation. Meanwhile, Zhou and Lin Biao went to meet Stalin in his dacha on 10–11 October. Eager to avoid a US–Soviet confrontation over Korea, Stalin insisted that the Soviet Union could not provide air cover for the Chinese ground forces operating in Korea but would supply abundant military equipment and materials. On 13 October, the Chinese Politburo made the final decision on sending Chinese troops to Korea without Soviet air cover. On 19 October, a quarter million Chinese People's Volunteers under the command of Peng Dehuai began to cross the Yalu River into North Korea.

Impact on Chinese–American–Soviet relations

Mao's decision to send troops to Korea turned China and America into hostile enemies. Confronted with 'an entirely new war' after the massive Chinese intervention in November/December, General MacArthur called for an extension of the war into China, and President Truman hinted at the use of nuclear weapons against Beijing. The United States intensified the political, economic, and military containment of China. It opposed Communist China's admission into the UN and imposed a trade embargo on China. On the other hand, the United States increased its military and economic commitment to Taiwan and accelerated the conclusion of a peace treaty with Japan, both of which were now regarded as key Cold War allies.[17]

In January 1951, the Chinese forces crossed the thirty-eighth parallel and captured the South Korean capital, Seoul. Following Beijing's rejection of various ceasefire proposals, on 1 February the United States secured the support of the UN to brand China an aggressor in Korea. On 18 May, the UN General Assembly voted in favour of a resolution recommending an embargo on strategic exports to China (and North Korea). Together with the export controls instituted by the Coordinating Committee of the Consultative Group comprising America and its European allies, China was prevented from acquiring a wide range of strategic materials, such as arms, petroleum, chemicals, and machinery.

While Sino-American relations deteriorated rapidly, the Korean War gave substance to the Sino-Soviet alliance. Despite Stalin's previous non-commitment to Soviet air support, in November the Soviet air force based in Manchuria was involved in defending the transportation lines across the Sino-Korean border. In January 1951 it engaged with US/UN aircraft over the northern part of North Korea. Above all, the Soviets supplied the bulk of arms and ammunition to China (although Beijing had to pay Moscow back after the war). Throughout the Korean conflict, Mao was in close and extensive consultation with Stalin. Mao decided to cross the thirty-eighth parallel in early 1951 after getting Stalin's full support. During the armistice talks between the Chinese/North Korean and US/UN representatives that began in July, Mao frequently sought the opinions and advice of Stalin.[18]

Sino-Soviet economic ties, too, were strengthened. The Korean War-related embargoes propelled Mao and his economic planners to speed up China's integration into the Soviet economic bloc. The patterns of China's export and import trade with the socialist and capitalist countries changed as a result. Between 1950 and 1952, the total volume of Sino-Soviet trade increased three-hold, from around US$338 million (29.8 per cent of China's total trade) to US$1,064 million (54.8 per cent). During the same period, China's trade with Britain, its largest capitalist trading partner, dropped from around US$73 to 25 million. China continued to acquire large quantities of Western goods via British Hong Kong through a combination of legal trade and illegal smuggling, however.[19]

Meanwhile, Mao seized upon the political and economic challenges of the Korean War to tighten state control over the society through a series of mass campaigns. Even before China's intervention in Korea, Mao and his comrades in charge of propaganda affairs had decided to adopt the slogan of 'Resist America and Assist Korea, and Defend our Home and our Country' to mobilize the Chinese people.[20] In late 1950 and early 1951, Mao launched the Campaign to Suppress Counter-revolutionaries in tandem with China's massive intervention in the Korean War. The campaign resulted in the arrest of more than 2.6 million people, with 712,000 'counter-revolutionaries' being executed.[21] Between late 1951 and 1952, the Three-Anti's Campaign (against corruption, waste, and excessive bureaucracy) and the Five-Anti's Campaign (against tax evasion, bribery, theft of state assets, cheating on government contracts, and stealing secret economic information) were underway. To Mao, China's involvement in the Korean War and the consolidation of state power through mass mobilization campaigns were inextricably linked.

Korean armistice

Negotiations over an armistice in Korea began on 10 July 1951 but it took almost two years to end the fighting.[22] During 1952, one of the most difficult issues to resolve was the exchange of prisoners of war (POW). While China and the Soviet Union demanded an all-for-all exchange, the United States insisted on the principle of voluntary repatriation. By May 1952 a stalemate over the POW issue ensued. What complicated the negotiation was the Communist propaganda campaign from early 1952 onwards that the United States was engaged in bacteriological warfare in North Korea and Manchuria. Washington, however, categorically denied it – and declassified Russian documents show that the campaign was based on fabricated evidence.[23]

Not until early 1953 was the impasse over the POW issue broken. In March China agreed to the American-proposed exchange of sick and wounded prisoners, and three months later, the principle of voluntary repatriation. That the CCP leadership was willing to compromise at this juncture was due to a number of factors. In late 1952, Dwight Eisenhower, who pledged to end the Korean War, had won the presidential election. After his inauguration, Eisenhower took a number of measures to put pressure on China, such as the 'unleashing' of Chiang Kai-shek and the threat of US nuclear attack. If the new leader in the White House was anxious to make peace, so was the new collective leadership in the Kremlin following Stalin's death in March. While the late Stalin had cautioned against compromise with the Americans, his successors wanted to relax international tension by ending the fighting in Korea.

Mao, too, felt that it was the time to conclude the three-year-long war in Korea. After all, China had already achieved military victory by fighting the United States to a standstill. China's international prestige had grown; it was recognized by both Washington and Moscow as a force to be reckoned with in Asia. Domestically, China needed a peaceful international environment to undertake its five-year plan of economic reconstruction.

Proletarian internationalism or national security?

What, then, was the main driving force behind China's entry into the Korean War? More generally, what was the main determinant of the PRC's approach to the outside world in its formative years? According to Chen Jian, who has made extensive use of Chinese archival material, ideology was more important than any other factors. To maintain the momentum of China's 'continuous revolution', Mao had long decided to commit Chinese troops to Korea. The US crossing of the thirty-eighth parallel and advance towards the Yalu River justified, rather than triggered, China's intervention in Korea. Believing that war was inevitable and the mountainous Korean peninsula was an ideal place for fighting, Mao and his Politburo decided to beat the 'American imperialists' there even without the promise of Soviet air cover for the Chinese troops.[24]

Allen Whiting and Simei Qing, on the other hand, argue that the US crossing of the thirty-eighth parallel played a critical role in Beijing's decision-making: the advance of American troops towards the Sino-Korean border did pose a genuine threat to China's national security that had to be countered. To Qing, who has been informed by Chinese archival sources, Mao had not pursued a 'confrontational policy' towards America and had not started military preparations prior to the Korean War. Nor had Mao issued the order to send troops to Korea (8 October) before the US crossing of the 38th parallel (7 October). Mao's approach to America was not influenced by the ideology of 'exporting revolution' as such but by the imperative of avoiding confrontation through a mix of moderation and deterrence. China's entry to the Korean War was not the result of inevitable Sino-American confrontation but of 'fatal misjudgments of each other's intentions in the time of crisis'.[25]

The 'ideology-versus-security' debate about China's involvement in the Korean War is bound to continue. It may well be argued that China intervened in Korea to define its new identity both as a communist state, which felt obliged to support its North Korean ally, and as a newly founded sovereign state, which placed a premium on national independence and territorial integrity. In developing diplomatic relations with the socialist and capitalist countries and annexing lost territories during 1949–53, China saw its identity in the same light.

Notes

1 The Ministry of Foreign Affairs and the CCP Central Committee's Party Literature Research Center (ed.), *Mao Zedong on Diplomacy* (Beijing: Foreign Languages Press, 1998), 89.
2 Han Nianlong *et al.*, *Diplomacy of Contemporary China* (Hong Kong: New Horizon Press, 1990), 11–12, 584.
3 On the Mao–Stalin talks in Moscow, see Sergei N. Goncharov, John W. Lewis, and Xue Litai, *Uncertain Partners: Stalin, Mao, and the Korean War* (Stanford: Stanford University Press, 1993), 76–129; Chen Jian, *Mao's China and the Cold War* (Chapel Hill: The University of North Carolina Press, 2001), 78–85.
4 On the main treaty, see Han *et al.*, op. cit., 491–3.
5 Goncharov, Lewis, and Xue, op. cit., 76, 98–100.
6 Han *et al.*, op. cit., 12–15.
7 Wenguang Shao, *China, Britain and Businessmen: Political and Commercial Relations, 1949–1957* (Basingstoke: Macmillan, 1991), 31–6.
8 Chi-kwan Mark, *Hong Kong and the Cold War: Anglo-American Relations, 1949–1957* (Oxford: Oxford University Press, 2004), 26–9.
9 See Chen Jian, 'The Chinese Communist "Liberation" of Tibet, 1949–51', in Jeremy Brown and Paul G. Pickowicz (eds), *Dilemmas of Victory: The Early Years of the People's Republic of China* (Cambridge, Mass.: Harvard University Press, 2007), 130–59.

10 Melvyn C. Goldstein, *A History of Modern Tibet, 1913–1951: The Demise of the Lamaist State* (Berkeley: University of California Press, 1989), 740.
11 Goncharov, Lewis, and Xue, op. cit., 148–52.
12 Kathryn Weathersby, 'The Soviet Role in the Korean War: The State of Historical Knowledge', in William Stueck (ed.), *The Korean War in World History* (Lexington: The University Press of Kentucky, 2004), 63–70.
13 On this theme, see Goncharov, Lewis, and Xue, op. cit.
14 Ibid., 145–6.
15 Roshchin to Filippov (Stalin), 3 October 1950, conveying Mao's message to Stalin, 2 October 1950, in *Cold War International History Project Bulletin* (hereafter *CWIHPB*) 6–7 (Winter 1995–6): 114–16. On an analysis of the two different versions of the 2 October message, see Shen Zhihua (trans. Chen Jian), 'The Discrepancy between the Russian and Chinese Versions of Mao's 2 October 1950 Message to Stalin on Chinese Entry into the Korean War: A Chinese Scholar's Reply', in *CWIHPB* 8–9 (Winter 1996–7): 237–42.
16 See Chen Jian, *China's Road to the Korean War: The Making of the Sino-American Confrontation* (New York: Columbia University Press, 1994), 171–209; Chen, *Mao's China and the Cold War*, 89–91.
17 See Qiang Zhai, *The Dragon, the Lion, and the Eagle: Chinese–British–American Relations, 1949–1958* (Kent, Ohio: The Kent State University Press, 1994), 89–112.
18 Chen Jian, 'China and the Korean War: New Findings and Perspectives in Light of New Documentation', in Mark F. Wilkinson (ed.), *The Korean War at Fifty: International Perspectives* (Lexington, Va.: Virginia Military Institute, 2004), 77–9.
19 See Shu Guang Zhang, *Economic Cold War: America's Embargo against China and the Sino-Soviet Alliance, 1949–1963* (Washington, D.C.: Woodrow Wilson Center Press, 2001), 79–112. Trade figures on 282, 289, 294.
20 Chen, *China's Road to the Korean War*, 190–4.
21 Yang Kuisong, 'Reconsidering the Campaign to Suppress Counter-revolutionaries', *CQ* 193 (March 2008): 102–21.
22 See William Stueck, *Rethinking the Korean War: A New Diplomatic and Strategic History* (Princeton: Princeton University Press, 2002), 143–81.
23 Kathryn Weathersby, 'Deceiving the Deceivers: Moscow, Beijing, Pyongyang, and the Allegations of Bacteriological Weapons Used in Korea', *CWIHPB* 11 (Winter 1998): 176–80.
24 Chen, *China's Road to the Korean War*.
25 Allen S. Whiting, *China Crosses the Yalu* (Stanford: Stanford University Press, 1968); Simei Qing, *From Allies to Enemies: Visions of Modernity, Identity, and US–China Diplomacy, 1945–1960* (Cambridge, Mass.: Harvard University Press, 2007), 151–68.

3 Peaceful coexistence and assertive nationalism, 1954–7

Shortly after the end of the Korean War, China's priorities shifted to state-building and economic rehabilitation. In October 1953 Mao Zedong adopted the 'general line for the transition to socialism'. In 1954 the National People's Congress approved a new constitution, modelled largely on the Soviet constitution of 1936. China's political system became a Leninist one, characterized by one-party rule, the cult of personality, and reliance on public security organs and propaganda techniques.

Meanwhile, China was integrated into a 'socialist world economy stretching from Berlin to Canton'. The CCP's First Five Year Plan (1953–7) emulated the Soviet plans in all aspects: centralized planning, an emphasis on heavy industry and military development, the nationalization of foreign trade, and the collectivization of agriculture. China fostered close economic links with the Soviet Union and its Eastern European satellites. The Soviets provided a considerable amount of aid (which needed to be repaid) and transferred technological knowhow (which was basically free) to China. More than 10,000 Soviet advisors arrived to assist in over 200 industrial projects. An even greater number of Chinese students and engineers went to the Soviet Union and Eastern European countries for education and training. China imported and translated thousands of Soviet books.[1] In sum, China learnt intensively from the Soviet Union in the mid-1950s. The learning was voluntary and whole-hearted, in contrast with the imposition of the Soviet model on the Eastern European 'People's Democracies' through military and political pressure.[2]

But domestic development required a peaceful international environment. In the mid-1950s, the Chinese leaders formulated the diplomacy of peaceful coexistence.

Peaceful coexistence diplomacy

The death of Stalin in March 1953 and the end of the Korean War in July that year propelled the Chinese leaders to reassess the changing balance of forces in the world. As Zhou Enlai observed in early June: 'The major contradiction in China's foreign policy is not the struggle between the socialist and the capitalist countries but [the contest] between war and peace.' In the post-Stalin era, the new Kremlin leaders called for the 'peaceful coexistence' of the socialist and capitalist systems to reduce international tensions. The conclusion of the Korean armistice demonstrated that the American superpower could not defeat a technologically backward China. In Zhou's assessment, the 'force of peace' in the world had been strengthened, and the imperialist powers would not be able to launch a world war in the near future. Due to the growing 'contradictions' within the imperialist camp, the United States was now a diminishing threat to China's security. Zhou believed that China could strengthen the forces of peace and cooperation in the world by exploiting the contradictions between the United States, which emphasized military alliances and war, and its allies in Europe and Asia as well as the peace-loving countries, which desired the relaxation of tensions.[3]

In 1954 Zhou formulated the Five Principles of Peaceful Coexistence as the guidance for China's foreign policy. They included 'mutual respect for each other's territorial integrity and sovereignty', 'mutual non-aggression', 'mutual non-interference in each other's internal affairs', 'equality and mutual benefit', and 'peaceful coexistence'. Although the essence of the Five Principles had been spelt out by Mao and other Chinese leaders since 1949, it was Zhou who creatively put them into practice.[4] While agreeing with the assessment that the force of peace had grown in China's favour, the ideological Mao disagreed with the pragmatic Zhou over the prospect of war with the American imperialists, which the Chairman believed was inevitable as long as class differences existed.[5] Nevertheless, confident of Zhou's diplomatic skills, and anxious to exploit the contradictions within the Western camp, Mao was willing to allow Zhou to pursue a conciliatory foreign policy in the mid-1950s.

Zhou's diplomatic initiative first focused on non-aligned India. On 29 April 1954, the PRC and India concluded an agreement on trade concerning Tibet based on the Five Principles; on 28 June, they formally endorsed the Principles in the Sino-Indian Agreement. Under Jawaharlal Nehru's leadership, India shared with China not only a long border, but also the common experience of Western colonialism and imperialism as well as a strong desire for peace. By upholding the banner of peaceful coexistence, Zhou identified China with the newly independent, non-aligned Asian countries in the Cold War struggle. (Following India, non-aligned Burma also endorsed the Five Principles.) In this regard,

Zhou conceived the strategy of peaceful coexistence as an international united front that provided for the strategic alignment of Chinese communism with Asian neutralism in the struggle against US imperialism.[6]

More importantly, Zhou was eager to apply the Five Principles to international relations, especially concerning the resolution of conflicts through peaceful negotiation. Such an opportunity came in early 1954, when the situation in Indochina deteriorated rapidly.

The Geneva Conference on Indochina

Since 1946, the Vietminh under Ho Chi Minh had been waging an anti-colonial struggle against the French in Indochina (consisting of Vietnam, Laos, and Cambodia). By 1953, the United States feared that the defeat of France in Indochina would produce a 'falling domino' effect on the whole of Southeast Asia as well as Japan. The Dwight Eisenhower administration provided massive economic and military aid to Paris. China, on the other hand, supported the Vietminh out of security and ideological considerations. Mao regarded Indochina as one of the three important but vulnerable fronts for China's physical security, the other two being Taiwan and Korea. It was imperative to make Indochina a buffer zone between China and the West. Ideologically, Mao felt strongly that China had a duty to help its fellow Communist countries and that the Chinese model of revolution was universally applicable to worldwide anti-colonial struggles. This was especially so for Vietnam, which had close historic and cultural ties with China, and for Ho, who had been involved in the Chinese Communist movement and the Sino-Japanese War. Nevertheless, Mao was anxious to avoid provoking US armed intervention in Indochina, especially after the outbreak of the Korean War. Thus, Beijing supported the Vietminh through the dispatch of Chinese military advisors and the provision of substantial ammunitions and financial aid. In August 1950 the Chinese Military Advisory Group was established in Vietnam; its roles included the training, planning, and even commanding of the Vietminh's military operations.[7]

In mid-March 1954, the Vietminh launched their offensive against the French garrisons at Dien Bien Phu, a remote village in a valley surrounded by high mountains in north-western Vietnam. Under siege, the French urgently requested Washington to launch air strikes to rescue them. Caught between the competing forces of anti-communism and anti-colonialism, the Eisenhower administration called for 'united action' with US allies and sympathetic countries. But most countries, especially Britain, wanted a diplomatic solution to the crisis. On 29 April,

Eisenhower decided against US unilateral intervention, and a few days later, the French forces in Dien Bien Phu collapsed.

On 8 May, the Geneva Conference convened to discuss the Indochina problem. Co-chaired by the Soviet Union and Britain, the Geneva Conference was the first international conference where the PRC was invited to participate on an equal basis with other powers. The main objective of Zhou, who headed the Chinese delegation of more than 200 members, was to achieve the neutralization of Indochina. He wanted to extend the 'zone of peace' in the immediate vicinity of China by removing the hostile foreign presence in Vietnam, Laos, and Cambodia.[8] From a broader perspective, Zhou saw the Geneva Conference as an essential test case for peaceful resolution of international conflicts under the Five Principles. By taking a moderate and conciliatory posture at Geneva, Zhou hoped to promote a benevolent image of China as a responsible player in international affairs. As a 'normal state', Zhou would then argue, China deserved recognition and respect but not containment and isolation by the US-led capitalist camp.[9]

But if the Chinese were eager to restore peace in Indochina, the Americans, pessimistic about reaching a favourable settlement, focused on organizing a collective security system consisting of the three Indochinese states as well as other friendly Asian countries. The US delegation to Geneva was instructed to assume an ambivalent yet uncompromising position, not playing an active role in the negotiation. (Its head, Secretary of State John Foster Dulles, even refused to shake hands with Premier Zhou when they encountered each other at the conference by chance.)

At Geneva, Zhou used his diplomatic skills to exploit the contradictions between America and its allies, France and Britain. In mid-June Pierre Mendes-France came to power in Paris and promised to reach a ceasefire within four weeks or else to resign. During the negotiations, the French/Americans and the Vietminh were divided over the question of a demarcation line of ceasefire (later partition) in Vietnam and the presence of foreign troops in Laos and Cambodia. To break the stalemate, Zhou met Mendes-France and Ho outside the conference room, persuading both sides to make concessions. By manipulating their strong desire for peace, Zhou hoped to split the realistic French from the adamant Americans. Zhou's shuttle diplomacy smoothed the way for the reaching of agreements.[10]

On 21 July, the Geneva Conference concluded with a set of accords and agreements, providing for an immediate ceasefire in Indochina, the partition of Vietnam along the seventeenth parallel, the holding of elections on Vietnamese unification in July 1956, and the withdrawal of all foreign forces from Laos and Cambodia. It was a diplomatic victory for China. The PRC had participated in its first ever international conference as an equal; Zhou had set a precedent for the peaceful resolution of international disputes under the Five Principles. It was a setback for the United States, though, which refused to sign the Geneva Accords but only unilaterally declared not to use force to upset it. To contain Communist expansion in the wake of Geneva, in September the United States signed the Manila Treaty with Britain, France, Australia, New Zealand, Pakistan, Thailand, and the Philippines, creating the Southeast Asia Treaty Organization (SEATO).

Assertive nationalism in the Taiwan Strait

On 3 September, China began the bombardment of the Nationalist-held offshore islands of Jinmen (Quemoy) and Mazu (Matsu), triggering an eight-month-long crisis in the Taiwan Strait. Why did Mao resort to military action at a time when Zhou tried to construct China's 'peaceful' image? To the Chairman, there was no contradiction between his 'tension diplomacy' in the Taiwan Strait and Zhou's calls for 'peaceful coexistence' with the West. Indeed, it was the Americans who had violated the Five Principles in the first place, making it necessary for China to reassert its principled position.[11] By forming the SEATO and establishing military bases and alliances with Asian countries, Mao accused the United States of having violated the principles of non-aggression and non-interference in other countries' internal affairs. By prohibiting trade with China and other Communist states, it had shown its contempt for mutual benefit and equality. Above all, by supporting the Nationalist regime and concluding a bilateral mutual defence treaty with Taiwan, which was suspected to be underway in the summer of 1954, Washington had infringed China's sovereignty over the island and undermined the territorial integrity of the PRC.

Mao thus approached the bombardment of the offshore islands from a broader strategic perspective.[12] It was a political move to focus world attention on China's sovereignty over Taiwan and America's encirclement of the PRC through military alliances and diplomatic isolation. Mao wanted to demonstrate to the world community that Taiwan was part of China and Beijing had every right to resolve by whatever means what it deemed an internal affair. A massive 'Liberate Taiwan' propaganda campaign thus preceded military bombardment, which was also aimed at domestic mobilization. From a tactical, military point of view, Mao planned to seize the Dachens (Tachens), an island group far to the north of Mazu and the weakest point in the Nationalist-held offshore island chain. In 1954 Mao had no intention to 'liberate' Jinmen and Mazu, let alone Taiwan and the Pescadores, a calculated delay which was in line with his strategy of recovering China's territories 'from small to large, one island at a time, from north to south, and from weak to strong'.[13]

But Mao's strategy backfired. Rather than prevent it, the bombardment gave impetus to the conclusion of the US–Taiwan defence treaty. The Eisenhower administration responded to the crisis with a two-pronged strategy. On the one hand, the United States expedited the negotiation over a mutual defence treaty with Taipei, under which Taiwan and the Pescadores would be protected. On the other, Washington sought the support of Britain and the Commonwealth to sponsor a ceasefire resolution in the UN to cover the offshore islands. On 12 December the US–Taiwan Mutual Defence Treaty was signed.

Mao reacted with the bombardment of Dachen Island in early January 1955, the heaviest attack since the crisis began. On 18 January the Chinese forces captured Yijiangshan, the largest island of the Dachen group. With little progress on the submission of a ceasefire solution to the UN – America and its allies were divided over the strategic value and thus defence needs of the offshore islands – the Eisenhower administration concluded that the GMD troops had better withdraw from the Dachens, and in return America would assist Taiwan in the defence of Jinmen and Mazu. Jiang reluctantly agreed. On 29 January, the US Congress passed the Formosa Resolution, which authorized the president to employ armed forces to protect Taiwan and the 'related areas'. By mid-February, the Nationalists completed their withdrawal from the Dachens.

In March Eisenhower apparently escalated the crisis by suggesting the use of atomic weapons in the same way as 'a bullet or anything else'. Eisenhower's nuclear threat did not immediately cause Mao to back down, although the Chairman did make the decision to build an atomic bomb around this time in order to avoid future US nuclear blackmail. Mao decided to end the First Taiwan Strait Crisis in late April in the course of the Bandung Conference for broader political reasons.

The Bandung Conference

The Afro-Asian Conference at Bandung between 18 and 24 April was attended by 29 newly independent Asian, African, and Middle Eastern countries. In response to the globalization and militarization of the Cold War, the five Colombo powers, the conference sponsors, hoped to cultivate goodwill and cooperation among the participating nations and to promote world peace. Accepting the invitation with great enthusiasm, China saw Bandung as a good opportunity to improve relations with its Asian neighbours suspicious of Beijing's territorial intentions. Like the Geneva Conference a year earlier, Zhou, who headed the Chinese delegation, wanted to portray China as a peaceful and responsible power in front of a large audience at Bandung. By demonstrating how the Five Principles of Peaceful Coexistence could contribute to world peace, Zhou hoped to discourage the Asian and African countries from participating in the American-led military alliances and collective defence organization.[14]

To Zhou, as all the participating Asian and African countries had suffered from different degrees of colonialism, they shared with China a strong desire for independence and justice. But Zhou was also acutely aware of the existing differences among the Afro-Asian countries. He estimated that the United States and the European colonial powers, which were excluded from the conference, would try to exploit the differences between the pro-Western, pro-alliance states (such as Turkey and Pakistan) and the non-aligned states (such as Indonesia and India). With a view to frustrating the possible American attempts to stir up endless debates by proxies, Zhou defined his approach at Bandung as 'seeking common ground while reserving differences'. Assuming a position of flexibility and reasonableness, the Chinese delegation would not quarrel with other conference participants but would preserve unity through consensus and concession.[15]

At Bandung, Zhou's conciliatory approach impressed many of the participants and helped to guide the conference in a more constructive direction. When the agenda item of 'promotion of world peace and cooperation' came up on 22–23 April, there was hot debate between the pro-alliance and pro-peaceful coexistence countries. On one side, Turkey justified the North Atlantic Treaty Organization as a system of self-defence; the Philippines argued that small and weak Southeast Asian states needed external protection; and Iraq attacked China's Five Principles as too vague. On the other side, both Indonesia and Egypt called for the end of military alliances and great power politics.[16] Reacting sharply and unyieldingly, India asserted that 'there is no alternative for any country, unless it wants war, but to accept the concept of peaceful coexistence'. Zhou's response was diplomatic and restrained: 'We should leave aside our different ideologies'; otherwise, 'our discussions will go on interminably and will prove fruitless ultimately'. If other countries found the term 'peaceful coexistence' unacceptable, Zhou proposed the expression 'Live together in peace'. At last, the Bandung Declaration, issued at the end of the conference, incorporated four of China's Five Principles (except for 'peaceful coexistence') into its Ten Principles. To Zhou, the Ten Principles were 'an extension and development of the five principles of peaceful coexistence'.[17]

Beyond the official proceedings, Zhou used the occasion of Bandung to reach out to other Asian leaders. Realizing that China's Asian neighbours were suspicious of its territorial and political intentions, Zhou reassured them through concessions. Zhou and the Indonesian President signed a treaty of dual nationality for overseas Chinese in Indonesia, according to which Beijing abandoned its presumed protection of the Chinese minority there and instead urged them to choose either Chinese or Indonesian nationality. Zhou sought to assure the Thais by inviting them to inspect the so-called 'Thai Autonomous Zone' in Yunnan, which allegedly harboured Thai opposition elements. Likewise, Zhou offered to conclude a non-aggression pact with the Philippines.

During his lunch meeting with the five Colombo Prime Ministers and other non-aligned leaders on 23 April, Zhou was asked whether China would attack the offshore islands. He replied by expressing his willingness to enter into negotiations with the Americans about relaxing tension in the Far East, thus de-escalating the ongoing Taiwan Strait Crisis. In September, Sino-American ambassadorial talks were held at Geneva (and later Warsaw), talks that would continue, on and off, for one and a half decades.

Sino-Soviet cooperation and conflict

In the mid-1950s, Sino-Soviet relations entered their 'golden years'.[18] After Stalin's death, Party First Secretary Nikita Khrushchev emerged as a key member of the collective leadership in the Kremlin. To struggle for supreme personal power, Khrushchev saw the need to strengthen Soviet power and influence on the world stage. He strove to achieve this by intensifying Sino-Soviet cooperation, which in turn required the removal of the 'unequal' aspects of the relationship. In late September and early October 1954, Khrushchev made his landmark visit to China and concluded a series of agreements with Mao. The Soviets agreed to return to China their military bases in Lushun, give up their shares in four joint ventures, increase Soviet loans to Beijing, and provide technological support for China's industrial projects.

In 1956 Khrushchev, having consolidated his leadership position, injected new elements into the dynamic of the Sino-Soviet relationship. During the Twentieth Party Congress of the Communist Party of the Soviet Union (CPSU) in February, Khrushchev made his so-called 'secret speech', in which he criticized Stalin's personality cult and policy excesses. In a thermonuclear age, he contended, war was no longer inevitable. Rather, Khrushchev called for the peaceful coexistence between capitalist and socialist countries, and suggested the possibility of a peaceful transition to socialism.

Mao was upset about the lack of consultation before Khrushchev delivered his 'de-Stalinization' speech. By criticizing Stalin's personality cult, Khrushchev also unwittingly undermined the similar kind of personality cult promoted by the Chairman himself. Mao felt that, for all his serious mistakes, Stalin remained a great Marxist-Leninist revolutionary leader. Above all, Mao disagreed strongly with Khrushchev's reinterpretation of Marxism-Leninism. To him, war with the American imperialists was inevitable, and there was no alternative to world revolution.

Notwithstanding his ideological disagreement with Khrushchev, Mao continued to regard the Soviet Union as the centre of the socialist bloc. Yet Mao could not but perceive himself as more morally paramount than the Soviet leader. The outbreak of political upheavals in Poland and Hungary in October intensified Mao's sense of moral superiority, and allowed China for the first time to play a key role in resolving crises in the international Communist movement. In Poland, after a series of worker strikes, Wladyslaw Gomulka returned to power on 19 October. He sought to eliminate pro-Soviet leaders within the government and declared he would pursue a Polish road to socialism. Khrushchev informed Beijing of his intention to send Soviet troops to restore order in Poland. To Mao, however, the Polish uprisings were caused by 'Soviet big-power chauvinism' – the Soviet domination of and discrimination against the Poles. Since the Polish crisis was basically anti-Soviet in nature, Mao opposed the use of force and instead wanted Moscow to address the problem by managing Soviet–Polish relations on the basis of equality. A CCP delegation led by Liu Shaoqi and Deng Xiaoping for consultation with Khrushchev arrived in Moscow on 23 October, by which time a crisis had already erupted in Hungary. In Mao's views, unlike the Polish uprisings, the crisis in Hungary was 'counterrevolutionary', which aimed to overthrow the socialist system and withdraw Hungary from the Warsaw Pact. Thus, Mao urged an indecisive Khrushchev, who vacillated between armed intervention and withdrawal, to re-send troops to crush the Hungarian uprisings in the interest of the socialist bloc.[19]

Khrushchev's 'de-Stalinization', then, was both a challenge and an opportunity for Mao. During 1957, the Soviet Union and China strengthened their cooperation in the military/nuclear field. In early

October the Soviet Union successfully launched *Sputnik*, the world's first satellite, into space, symbolizing its advantage in missile technology. The same month, Moscow concluded with Beijing a secret nuclear cooperation agreement, which provided for the supply of a prototype atomic bomb to China. Mao in turn lent his political support to Khrushchev. At the Moscow Conference attended by 64 of the world Communist and workers' parties in November, Mao, as co-sponsor, played a key role in hammering out the Moscow Declaration (signed by the 12 Communist parties in power) which endorsed the decisions of the Twentieth Congress of the CPSU.

Nevertheless, the year 1957 closed with a significant radicalization of Mao's thinking and the accumulation of hidden tensions in the Sino-Soviet alliance. At home, Mao had reversed the earlier Hundred Flowers Campaign, which encouraged intellectuals and technical experts to criticize the political system in order to improve it, by launching the Anti-Rightist Campaign against those who had spoken out against the Party. The Soviet launch of *Sputnik* had so strengthened Mao's confidence in the strength of the socialist camp that he declared 'the East Wind prevails over the West Wind'. Mao became impatient and sceptical about Zhou's diplomacy of peaceful coexistence. By the end of 1957, the Sino-American ambassadorial talks had made no progress on the Taiwan question and were downgraded by Washington. Lastly, while the Moscow Conference of November 'marked the peak of Sino-Soviet alliance relations', according to two Chinese historians, it 'was also, in some sense, the turning point in the relationship'. At Moscow, a confident Mao had spoken assertively on the Soviet intra-party struggle, the benefits of a nuclear war, and China's prospects for overtaking Britain within 15 years and catching up with America a little later, all of which indicated his aspirations to be the leader of the international Communist movement.[20]

The 'peaceful coexistence' phase of Chinese foreign policy was thus brought to an abrupt end. In 1958 Mao was redefining China's identity and role on the world stage that better reflected his radicalized domestic and foreign policy agenda.

Empty rhetoric or genuine principles?

Were the Five Principles of Peaceful Coexistence merely empty slogans? Did they retain significance in Chinese foreign policy after 1957? By highlighting the instrumental use of the Five Principles by the Chinese leaders, some scholars may have suggested the answer. To Ronald Keith, Zhou and Mao conceived the strategy of peaceful coexistence in the context of an international united front to ally China with the Asian neutralist states and the pragmatic Western countries in the struggle against the main enemy, the United States.[21] According to Chih-Yu Shih, the rhetoric of 'peace' was employed as a 'shaming technique'. By calling for 'peaceful coexistence' with the United States, which Mao predicted would most likely not reciprocate, China could dramatize how the American imperialists had violated the world community's peace expectations.[22]

Wang Jisi, looking from the perspective of Chinese culture, argues that 'peaceful coexistence' was not simply self-righteous rhetoric to serve propaganda purposes but was indeed rooted in Confucian tradition and Chinese moralist thinking. The Chinese believed that if everyone acted morally, the collective goodwill of mankind could be advanced. When it came to international relations, if all states exercised moral restraint according to the Five Principles, friendly relations and world peace could be achieved.[23] In a case study on China–Cambodia relations with broader implications for China's foreign relations, Sophie Richardson argues that the Five Principles were not empty rhetoric but 'a clear Chinese articulation of its expectations about and obligations to international relations'. As an impoverished, undeveloped country, China was ideologically committed to global revolutionary change. But what was at stake was not specifically about the export of Marxist revolution to every corner of the world. Rather, it was about 'freedom of states to choose their own systems, to engage in equitable bilateral and multilateral relations, and to stave off major conflicts'.[24]

It is true that, although the Chinese leaders attacked rather than advocated peaceful coexistence with America after 1957, the other four of the Five Principles such as national sovereignty and mutual benefits continued to guide China's foreign policy, up to the present. They were enduring ideals and core values that lay at the heart of China's search for a new national identity after 1949.

Notes

1 William C. Kirby, 'China's Internationalization in the Early People's Republic: Dreams of a Socialist World Economy', *CQ* 188 (December 2006), especially 882–7.

2 Thomas P. Bernstein, 'Introduction: The Complexities of Learning from the Soviet Union', in Thomas P. Bernstein and Hua-yu Li (eds), *China Learns from the Soviet Union, 1949–Present* (Lanham: Rowman & Littlefield, 2010), 5.

3 Xiaohong Liu, *Chinese Ambassadors: The Rise of Diplomatic Professionalism since 1949* (Hong Kong: Hong Kong University Press, 2001), 53–4.

4 Zhang Baijia, 'Zhou Enlai – The Shaper and Founder of China's Diplomacy', in Michael H. Hunt and Niu Jun (eds), *Toward a History of Chinese Communist Foreign Relations, 1920s–1960s: Personalities and Interpretative Approaches* (Washington, D.C.: Woodrow Wilson International Center for Scholars, 1995), 83.

5 Liu, op. cit., 55.

6 Ronald C. Keith, *The Diplomacy of Zhou Enlai* (London: Macmillan, 1989), 116–17.

7 Qiang Zhai, *China and the Vietnam Wars, 1950–1975* (Chapel Hill: The University of North Carolina Press, 2000), 10–42; Chen Jian, 'China and the First Indo-China War, 1950–54', *CQ* 133 (March 1993): 85–110.

8 Shao Kuo-kang, 'Zhou Enlai's Diplomacy and the Neutralization of Indochina, 1954–55', *CQ* 107 (September 1986): 483–504.

9 On this theme, see Shu Guang Zhang, 'Constructing "Peaceful Coexistence": China's Diplomacy toward the Geneva and Bandung Conferences, 1954–55', *CWH* 7: 4 (November 2007): 509–28.

10 Zhai, op. cit., 49–63.

11 Zhang Baijia, 'The Changing International Scene and Chinese Policy toward the United States, 1954–70', in Robert S. Ross and Jiang Changbin (eds), *Re-examining the Cold War: U.S.–China Diplomacy, 1954–1973* (Cambridge, Mass.: Harvard University Press, 2001), 50.

12 See Gordon H. Chang and He Di, 'The Absence of War in the U.S.–China Confrontation over Quemoy and Matsu in 1954–55: Contingency, Luck, Deterrence?', *American Historical Review* 98: 5 (December 1993): 1500–24; Shu Guang Zhang, *Deterrence and Strategic Culture: Chinese–American Confrontations 1949–1958* (Ithaca: Cornell University Press, 1992), 189–224.

13 Quoted in He Di, 'The Evolution of the People's Republic of China's Policy toward the Offshore Islands', in Warren I. Cohen and Akira Iriye (eds), *The Great Powers in East Asia 1953–1960* (New York: Columbia University Press, 1990), 223.

14 Keith, op. cit., 81.

15 The Theoretical Study Group of the Ministry of Foreign Affairs, *We Will Always Remember Chou En-lai* (Peking: Foreign Languages Press, 1977), 52–3.

16 Roeslan Abdulgani, *The Bandung Connection: The Asian–African Conference in Bandung in 1955* (Singapore: Gunung Agung, 1981), 137–48.

17 *China and the Asian–African Conference: Documents* (Peking: Foreign Languages Press, 1955), 56–62, 64–72.

18 For this section, I relied on Chen Jian, *Mao's China and the Cold War* (Chapel Hill: The University of North Carolina Press, 2001), 61–71.

19 Ibid., 145–62. On the Polish crisis, Lorenz M. Luthi has dismissed Mao's influence on Khrushchev by arguing that the Soviet leader had made up his own mind to halt, though not call off, the advance of Soviet troops. *The Sino-Soviet Split: Cold War in the Communist World* (Princeton: Princeton University Press, 2008), 54–7.

20 Zhihua Shen and Yafeng Xia, 'Hidden Currents during the Honeymoon: Mao, Khrushchev, and the 1957 Moscow Conference', *JCWS* 11: 4 (Fall 2009): 74–117.

21 Keith, op. cit.

22 Chih-Yu Shih, *China's Just World: The Morality of Chinese Foreign Policy* (Boulder: Lynne Rienner Publishers, 1993), 105.
23 Wang Jisi, 'International Relations Theory and the Study of Chinese Foreign Policy: A Chinese Perspective', in Thomas W. Robinson and David Shambaugh (eds), *Chinese Foreign Policy: Theory and Practice* (Oxford: Clarendon Press, 1995), 493, 501–2.
24 Sophie Richardson, *China, Cambodia, and the Five Principles of Peaceful Coexistence* (New York: Columbia University Press, 2010), 12–13.

4   Ideological radicalization and the Sino-Soviet split, 1958–64

By early 1958, Mao became dissatisfied with the state of China's economic development, and the Soviet model that inspired it. The collectivization of agriculture had not significantly increased the level of productivity in the countryside. The Chairman did not feel comfortable with a large state bureaucracy, centralized planning, concentration on heavy industry, and above all China's over-dependence on the Soviet Union. To Mao, China needed a much quicker and a more self-reliant path to communism: his solution was the launching of the Great Leap Forward. Mao held the conviction that China could overcome its technological backwardness and increase its agricultural and industrial production through the total mobilization of its 650 million population. It was the human will, not technology, that mattered.

As far as agricultural production was concerned, Mao intended to amalgamate the existing cooperatives/collectives into much bigger people's communes, each comprising more than 5,000 households. To achieve rapid industrialization, the Chinese people were mobilized in military style for large-scale public works and especially for the production of steel in their own back yard. By 'walking on two legs' – developing agriculture and industry simultaneously – China would make significant leaps in economic production and surpass the Western industrialized countries within a short space of time, or so Mao believed.

Mao's ideological radicalization was also manifested in the domestic political realm. In early 1958, in a number of central and provincial Party meetings chaired by him, Mao intensified his criticism of Zhou Enlai (and other CCP leaders) who had opposed 'rash advance' in China's economic development in the previous two years. Mao was also critical of Zhou's diplomacy of peaceful coexistence, especially concerning ambassadorial talks with the Americans which had achieved little effect. In consequence, Zhou stepped down as foreign minister (with the official explanation of concentrating on his premiership) and was asked to make self-criticism about his 'conservative and rightist tendency' in handling China's foreign policy.[1]

It is clear that Mao wanted to radicalize China's foreign policy, which was inextricably linked to the success of the Great Leap Forward. Mao needed international tensions for the sake of domestic mobilization.

Deteriorating Sino-Soviet relations

Between 1958 and 1962, Sino-Soviet relations were in a downward spiral. In mid-April 1958, the Soviet Defence Minister communicated to his Chinese counterpart Moscow's desire to construct a long-wave radio receiving station in China in order to facilitate long-distance communication with Soviet submarines in the Pacific region. Sensitive to the issue of national sovereignty, Mao saw the proposal as Moscow's attempt to control China. A few months later, the Soviets made another proposal to the Chinese, the construction of a joint Soviet–Chinese submarine flotilla. When Khrushchev visited Beijing between 31 July and 3 August, Mao expressed his strong reservations about the two proposals, describing them as manifestations of 'Soviet big-power chauvinism'. After four days of hard bargaining, the two sides finally reached an agreement on the construction of long-wave stations, with Moscow providing the finance and expertise and with Beijing retaining the ownership. In short, although the Soviets might not have intended to infringe upon China's sovereignty, Mao's 'victim mentality', grounded in the memory of the 'century of humiliation', contributed to his deep mistrust of foreign countries and over-sensitivity to real and perceived enemies.[2]

Khrushchev, for his part, was concerned about Mao's restless foreign policy adventure. On 23 August China started the bombardment of Jinmen and Mazu, triggering the Second Taiwan Strait Crisis. Mao aimed to stop the Nationalist harassment of the China coast from the offshore islands, put pressure on Washington, demonstrate China's solidarity with the anti-colonial struggles in the Middle East, and, most importantly, mobilize the Chinese people for the Great Leap Forward. The United States responded by reinforcing the Seventh Fleet in the Taiwan Strait and convoying Nationalist supplies to Jinmen. Worried that Washington would persuade Taipei to withdraw from Jinmen and Mazu, on 25 October Mao ended the crisis by calling for the Taiwanese compatriots to enter into peaceful unification talks, while continuing the bombardment of the offshore islands (on a much smaller scale) on alternate days. Mao justified his de-escalation as a 'noose' (*jiaosuo*) strategy of leaving the offshore islands in Nationalist hands in order to maintain the last physical link between Taiwan and mainland China.[3]

To Khrushchev, Mao's initiation of the Second Taiwan Strait Crisis was a challenge to the Soviet policy of peaceful coexistence with the United States. During his meeting with Mao in Beijing prior to the crisis in late July/early August, Khrushchev had not been informed of the impending bombardment. The intensification of the Great Leap Forward campaigns around the time of the crisis widened further the ideological and personal gap between the two leaders. Whereas Mao zealously claimed that China would enter the stage of communism before the Soviet Union, Khrushchev criticized the Great Leap Forward as a deviation from the Soviet economic model.[4]

But by the spring of 1959, it became clear that China's economy had not leapt forward but backward. There were severe food shortages in almost every province and administrative entity, affecting (for the whole year) as many as 25 million people with 310,000 of them estimated to have died of famine. The problem was caused to some extent by natural disasters but mainly by Mao's errors – the fanatical back-yard furnace movement (which produced useless pig iron rather than steel) at the expense of agricultural production, China's exports of grain to finance the speedy repayment of Soviet debts, and Mao's initial denial of the existence of famines. The situation had become so bleak that a reluctant Mao agreed to reduce production targets particularly that of steel. Mao stepped down as state president (while maintaining his Party chairmanship) and turned over economic management to pragmatic leaders such as Chen Yun, Deng Xiaoping, and Liu Shaoqi. Besides, he called a meeting of all central and provincial leaders at Lushan, Jiangxi, to discuss the challenges of the Great Leap Forward.[5]

The Lushan Conference, opened on 2 July, had an adverse impact on the Sino-Soviet relationship: it reinforced Mao's suspicions of the connection between domestic politics and international development, and between CCP opponents and the Soviet revisionists. On 14 July, Defence Minister Peng Dehuai wrote to Mao, suggesting a careful evaluation of the 'losses and achievements' of the Great Leap Forward. Mao discerned an 'international background' behind Peng's attack, coming as it did shortly after the latter's visit to the Soviet Union and Eastern European countries. Rather than addressing the problems caused by the Great Leap Forward, Mao used the Lushan Conference as a platform to denounce Peng's 'anti-party plot'. It is debatable whether Mao genuinely believed in a Peng–Khrushchev conspiracy against him. But it is clear that the Chairman was anxious to manipulate the alleged Soviet connection to discredit his political rivals within the Party who opposed the Great Leap Forward.[6]

Sino-Soviet relations were also affected by the Sino-Indian border clashes in August. Earlier in March, a rebellion had broken out in

Lhasa, Tibet, which was caused by the widespread unrest in 'ethnographic Tibet' (the ethnically Tibetan regions of Sichuan) in 1957–8. After suppressing the Lhasa rebellion, Beijing ended the autonomous status of Tibet under the 1951 Seventeen-Point Agreement, and the Dalai Lama and his supporters fled Lhasa and found refuge in India.[7] Together with renewed border disputes, on 25 August the Chinese and Indian forces clashed along the border. (Another armed clash occurred in late October.) Moscow adopted a position of 'neutrality' between Beijing and New Delhi, and issued a public statement regretting the outbreak of hostilities. To Mao, not only was Moscow's 'neutrality' a betrayal of its socialist ally, but its public statement had revealed, for the first time, the existence of Sino-Soviet dispute to a world audience.

The pursuit of US–Soviet détente pushed Sino-Soviet relations to the breaking point. Before the Eisenhower–Khrushchev summit at Camp David, scheduled for 15–27 September, Moscow had informed Beijing on 20 June that the Soviet Union, owing to the US–Soviet negotiations over the nuclear test ban, would no longer be able to provide China with assistance on nuclear technology. In other words, the Soviets had rescinded the 1957 nuclear agreement with China. Although the Eisenhower–Khrushchev summit failed to make any breakthrough on the German question, the two leaders exchanged views on a range of issues including China.

Encouraged by what he called the 'Camp David' spirit, Khrushchev set foot onto Chinese soil on 30 September to celebrate the tenth anniversary of the founding of the People's Republic. That day, Khrushchev argued that it was unwise to test the strength of the capitalist camp by military means. In the course of his five-day visit, Khrushchev spoke explicitly of Mao's 'adventurism' regarding Taiwan and India, complaining that China's actions threatened Moscow's policy of peaceful coexistence. He expressed sympathy for Peng and urged Mao to rehabilitate his former defence minister. Khrushchev delivered a message from Eisenhower to the Chinese leaders, requesting the release of five American prisoners on the mainland. To Mao, the founding of the PRC was a historic event, and its tenth anniversary a moment of pride and celebration. But to his astonishment, Khrushchev had come to China to talk about 'peaceful coexistence' with America rather than socialist solidarity, and to criticize Beijing's policy towards Taiwan rather than apologizing for the lack of Soviet support concerning India. Personally, Mao felt insulted by Khrushchev's offensive remarks.[8]

By early 1960, both the CCP and the CPSU claimed to represent real Marxism–Leninism, and resorted to polemics to win over other related parties in the struggle for the leadership of the international Communist movement. Beijing seized upon the hundredth anniversary of Lenin's birth to start its open assault on the Soviet Union by publishing three articles collectively entitled 'Long Live Leninism'. The first one, published in *Hongqi* on 16 April, launched a veiled attack on Khrushchev by accusing Tito of 'revisionism'. The other articles accused the 'revisionists' of betraying Leninism by advocating peaceful coexistence and a peaceful transition to socialism. Moscow's propaganda machine countered the Chinese attacks with its own articles.[9] The bottom line for both parties, however, was to keep the polemics indirect by not mentioning the other by name.

The breakdown of the Paris Summit between America, Britain, France, and the Soviet Union in May 1960 provided the CCP with ammunition for propagating the correctness of its ideology and policy. On 1 May, two weeks before the scheduled summit, an American U-2 spy plane was brought down over Soviet territory, with its pilot being captured and admitting spying. Accusing the American spy plane of violating Soviet airspace, Khrushchev demanded an apology from Eisenhower in Paris. When Eisenhower refused, the Paris Summit was aborted in acrimony. In China, the *People's Daily* published editorials denouncing Washington's provocation of the Soviet Union and thus the entire socialist bloc; mass rallies were held calling for Khrushchev's tough reaction.[10]

The ideological battles between the CCP and CPSU became more direct and public in late June. During the Congress of the Romanian Workers' Party and later the Bucharest Conference of the World Communist and Workers' Parties, Khrushchev seized the initiative to attack Mao's position. The communiqué of the Bucharest Conference endorsed the CPSU's views on the non-inevitability of war and the possibility of peaceful transition to socialism. While agreeing to sign the communiqué, on Mao's instructions the Chinese delegation issued a statement at Bucharest, criticizing Khrushchev by name and accusing the Soviets of launching a surprise attack on the CCP.[11]

Khrushchev retaliated by economic means. On 16 July, without prior consultation, Moscow informed Beijing that all Soviet advisors and experts in China would be withdrawn. What triggered the Soviet decision were Beijing's attempts to indoctrinate Soviet military specialists along its ideological line. By the end of August, approximately 1,400 Soviet personnel left China, and more than 200 projects of scientific and technological cooperation were scrapped. According to Lorenz Luthi, the overall negative effect on the Chinese economy was insignificant, for few Soviet experts had been involved in agricultural production and the economic situation was already very bad before the Soviet with-drawal.[12] Although the economic impact might have been minor, the unilateral and sudden nature of the Soviet decision hurt the feelings of Mao and other CCP leaders. To them, the Soviet Union had once again treated China in terms of a 'father-and-son relationship' rather than helping its ally to achieve economic modernization and great power status.[13] Ironically, Mao found the withdrawal of Soviet experts a convenient pretext to blame Moscow for China's economic collapse generally and in particular the severe famines, which were allegedly caused by the Soviet demand for instant repayment of debts. (Indeed, Mao himself decided to repay the debts of 1,407 million roubles within two years rather than the agreed 16 years by increasing exports of grain, cotton, and other raw materials.)[14]

Notwithstanding the ideological polemics and the breakdown of economic relations, both Mao and Khrushchev wanted to preserve unity, or at least to contain the Sino-Soviet rift through a semblance of unity – but for different reasons. By late 1960, it became clear even to Mao that China had witnessed the worst famine in what would be the 'three bitter years' (1959–61) of the Great Leap Forward. Pragmatic leaders such as Zhou, Liu, and Deng felt that a further deterioration of Sino-Soviet relations would not only worsen the economy but also affect China's national security. Indeed, China's peripheral security environment had little room for complacency, with the border tensions with India and the deteriorating situation in Laos and Vietnam.[15] As for Khrushchev, the U-2 incident and the aborted Paris Summit had dealt a great blow to his policy of détente with America, thereby providing an incentive for him to seek reconciliation with Beijing.

The holding of the Conference of World Communist and Workers' Parties in Moscow in November provided a chance for the CCP and the CPSU to seek rapprochement. But it was not going to be an easy task: the Chinese delegation, led by Liu and Deng, exchanged hostile words with the Soviets in the early stage of the proceedings. Ho Chi Minh played a role in mediating between the two Communist giants in the hope of uniting them against America and South Vietnam. At last, the Moscow Declaration reaffirmed the decisions of the CPSU's Twentieth Congress, recognized the danger of dogmatism and sectarianism, and confirmed the Soviet Union's leading position in the socialist bloc.[16]

But the Moscow Declaration was only 'a cosmetic truce'.[17] The emergence of the Soviet–Albanian split and China's sympathy towards the latter's side again pitted the CPSU against the CCP. During the Twenty-second Congress of the CPSU in October 1961, the Soviets resumed their indirect assault on China by criticizing Albania, Beijing's main supporter in the polemics, by name. The fundamental differences between the two parties remained irreconcilable.

Leftist trends in Chinese foreign policy since 1962

Since mid-1962, China's foreign policy was influenced by 'leftist' tendencies, thanks to the political comeback of Mao in day-to-day policy-making. Mao was unhappy about the pragmatic economic policies pursued by Liu and Deng, which he feared would bring about the 'restoration of capitalism' in China. As usual, the Chairman perceived a close connection between the domestic threat and the external one: the Chinese 'revisionists' were colluding with the revisionist Khrushchev to subvert China's 'continuous revolution' from within.[18]

The policy debate within the CCP leadership in the spring of 1962 heightened Mao's sense of the danger of a 'capitalist restoration', propelling him to re-emphasize class struggle in both domestic and foreign policy. The debate was triggered by Wang Jiaxiang, Director of the International Liaison Department of the CCP Central Committee and a 'Kremlinologist' who had studied in Moscow and served as the PRC's first ambassador to the Soviet Union. Concerned about the state of the Chinese economy, on 27 February Wang sent a letter to Zhou, Deng, and Chen Yi, suggesting ways to reduce tensions between China and the two superpowers as well as India. To Wang, it was wrong to overstress the danger of a world war and to underestimate the possibility of peaceful coexistence with the West. With regard to national liberation movements, Wang called for restraint and, if necessary, assistance within the confines of China's limited resources. Mao disagreed strongly with Wang, however. Criticizing Wang for advocating a 'revisionist line' of 'three moderations (towards imperialism, revisionism, and international reactionaries) and one reduction (of assistance to national liberation movements)', Mao wanted the Party to emphasize 'three struggles and one more'. That is to say, China should struggle against the imperialists, revisionists and reactionaries at home and abroad, as well as provide more assistance to national liberation fighters around the world.[19]

Mao's threat perceptions were heightened by international events in 1962. In May–June a war scare developed in the Taiwan Strait. In view of the famine in China and the public rift between Beijing and Moscow, Chiang Kai-shek believed that the time was ripe for his 'return to the mainland'. Chiang lobbied Washington to provide military aircraft and pilot training as well as supporting Taiwan's sabotage operations against China. By April–May 1962, the massive influx of Chinese refugees from the mainland to Hong Kong (an estimated total of 120,000) seemed to suggest the impending collapse of the Communist regime, causing Chiang to intensify war preparations. The Third Taiwan Strait Crisis had started. Mao responded with a deterrent strategy: the CCP Central Military Commission ordered the early implementation of the conscription plan and the PLA moved a massive number of troops and aircraft into Fujian opposite Taiwan. But neither Beijing nor Washington wanted war. The Guangdong authorities worked with the Hong Kong government to stop the exodus of Chinese refugees, while the US administration indicated to China that it opposed the use of force in the Taiwan Strait. The crisis thus ended as dramatically as it had begun.[20]

A more serious threat to China's sovereignty and territorial integrity came from India in October. After the 1959 clashes, Sino-Indian relations remained tense, notwithstanding the opening of border talks. By the summer of 1962, Nehru's 'forward policy' in the Himalayas resulted in renewed tensions and skirmishes between Indian and Chinese patrols in both the disputed eastern sector (the McMahon line) and western sector (the Aksai Chin) of the border. Beijing, moreover, was concerned about the perceived Indian subversive activities in Tibet. To 'teach India a lesson', China went for a limited war. On 20 October, the PLA struck at both sectors of the Sino-Indian border, advancing for a week and then pausing for three weeks before resuming the offensive. On 21 November, having defeated and humiliated India, China unilaterally announced a ceasefire and restored the status quo of 1959.[21]

Significantly, the Sino-Indian Border War coincided with another international crisis – the Cuban Missile Crisis. On 22 October, President John F. Kennedy announced that the Soviet Union had built nuclear missile sites in Cuba for the deployment of intermediate range ballistic missiles. Under intense pressure from Washington, Khrushchev had no choice but to agree, on the twenty-eighth, to withdraw the Soviet missiles from Cuba (in return for Kennedy's promise not to invade Cuba). After his humiliating climb-down over Cuba, Khrushchev announced a position of 'neutrality' in the ongoing Sino-Indian war, calling for a ceasefire and reversing the decision to suspend the supply of MIG-21 aircraft to New Delhi. To Mao, the Soviet Union had once again failed to honour its treaty obligations in war. Beijing, through propaganda and mass rallies, condemned the Soviet Union for 'capitulationism' during the Cuban Missile Crisis. By manipulating Khrushchev's policy blunders, Mao also had domestic political aims in mind – to discredit those CCP leaders who advocated a conciliatory foreign policy line or harboured hopes for 'capitalist restoration' such as Wang, Liu, and Deng.[22]

The Cuban Missile Crisis, which brought the superpowers to the nuclear brink, gave impetus to nuclear test ban negotiations. On 5 August 1963 in Moscow, America, the Soviet Union, and Britain signed the Partial Nuclear Test Ban Treaty. Beijing criticized it as the superpowers' attempts to monopolize nuclear weapons, at a time when China was producing its first nuclear bomb. Between September and July 1964, Mao published nine open letters, criticizing Khrushchev and his policies as 'phoney communism' in the most degrading terms. The Sino-Soviet polemics were brought to the widest possible world audience. The sudden downfall of Khrushchev in October and the ascent of Leonid Brezhnev did not fundamentally change the inherent structural problems of the Sino-Soviet alliance.

Relations with the 'two intermediate zones'

With the virtual collapse of the Sino-Soviet alliance, Mao identified China with the Asian, African, and Latin American countries in international affairs. Sharing the same experience of foreign imperialism, China always had an imagined 'Third World identity'. Indeed, the People's Republic from its inception was eager to develop diplomatic relations with other underdeveloped countries, beginning with its Asian neighbours. With accelerated decolonization in Africa since 1960, there was a second wave of diplomatic recognition: between 1960 and the end of 1965, a total of 16 Asian–African–Latin American states established diplomatic relations with the PRC.

By 1963 the newly independent countries took on a new strategic significance in Mao's eyes: they were conceived as part of an international anti-imperialist united front. Between September 1963 and early 1964, Mao crystallized his thinking into the concept of 'two intermediate zones'. Accordingly, there were 'two intermediate zones' in the world separating the United States from the Soviet Union: the first zone consisted of 'economically backward countries in Asia, Africa and Latin America' and the second zone 'imperialist and advanced countries' represented by Europe, Japan, and Canada. All these states had 'contradictions' with the two superpowers and did not want to be controlled by either Washington or Moscow.[23] As part of the 'first intermediate zone', Mao argued, China was the leader of the wars of national liberation in the Third World and the centre of world revolution.

In constructing an international united front against imperialism and revisionism, Beijing turned to the radical nationalist parties and states such as Egypt, Algeria, Cuba, and Indonesia. In mid-1964, following a preparatory meeting at Djakarta attended by 22 Afro-Asian countries, the newly created Organization of African Unity decided to convene a second Afro-Asian conference, with Algeria as the host. But from the outset, there were serious disagreements about which countries should be invited. China wanted to radicalize the Afro-Asian movement by excluding the Soviet Union from the conference. But India was anxious to prevent possible Chinese dominance of the conference and to channel the Asian-African countries to the Non-Aligned Movement, founded in 1961, of which it was a key member. Thus, India supported the invitation of the Soviet Union and of Malaysia, which was at odds with pro-Beijing Indonesia. The opinions were so divided that, when Algerian leader Ahmed Ben Bella was overthrown on 19 June 1965, the majority of the Afro-Asian states conveniently postponed the second Afro-Asian conference indefinitely.[24]

Besides, China cultivated relations with the countries in the 'second intermediate zone'. Eager to increase France's international prestige, demonstrate its independence from America, and secure a future role in the Third World, President Charles de Gaulle sought to establish diplomatic relations with the PRC. The end of the Algerian war of independence in 1962 and France's refusal to accede to the 1963 Partial Nuclear Test Ban Treaty smoothed the path for a Sino-French rapprochement. But the main obstacle was France's political links with Taiwan. Nonetheless, in order to make a diplomatic breakthrough in Western Europe, China adopted a flexible attitude towards the specific steps in establishing diplomatic relations as long as the principle of 'one China' was upheld. Accordingly, it agreed that France would first announce the recognition of the PRC as the sole legal government of China, and then sever diplomatic relations with Taiwan upon the latter's withdrawal of its diplomatic representative from Paris. On 27 January 1964, China and France issued a joint communiqué, announcing the establishment of diplomatic relations and the exchange of ambassadors within three months. Confronted with a political fait accompli, Taiwan closed its embassy in France.[25]

China's status on the world stage was further enhanced on 16 October, when it successfully exploded an atomic bomb. Although Mao had dubbed nuclear weapons 'paper tigers', he strongly felt that the PRC should join the world's exclusive nuclear club so as to demonstrate its great power status and prevent future nuclear blackmail by the superpowers. In line with Mao's thinking that all things had dual aspects, the nuclear weapons were both 'paper' and 'real tigers', to be despised from a strategic viewpoint but taken into full account tactically.[26]

Ideological split or power struggle?

Why did China break up with the Soviet Union and reassert its Third World identity by 1964? One line of explanation is Sino-Soviet ideological differences. According to Lorenz Luthi, ideology served a dual role, in that, while Mao genuinely believed in the correctness of his interpretation of Marxism-Leninism, he very often used ideology instrumentally to undermine his domestic political opponents, perceived and real. Thus, in 1959 Mao exploited the alleged Soviet connection to discredit those CCP leaders who opposed the Great Leap Forward such as Peng; in 1962 his criticism of Khrushchev was aimed to avert 'capitalist restoration' in China and to promote his radical foreign policy agenda. Mao's ideological radicalization since 1959 was thus the most decisive factor for the Sino-Soviet split. Chen Jian, also emphasizing the role of ideology, argues that the Sino-Soviet dispute was closely related to Mao's efforts to maintain the momentum of 'continuous revolution'. But unlike Luthi, who put the blame squarely on Mao, Chen equally blamed Khrushchev for pushing Sino-Soviet relations to breaking point by arrogantly treating the Chinese Chairman who was held captive by his own 'victim mentality'.[27]

Another interpretation holds that the Sino-Soviet dispute was primarily a clash of national interests, not of ideologies. The abrogation of the Sino-Soviet nuclear agreement in 1959, the withdrawal of Soviet experts from the mainland in 1960, and the conclusion of the 1963 Partial Nuclear Test Ban Treaty had practical security and economic consequences for the PRC. Wang Dong argues that, despite ideological differences, Mao was eager to avoid a Sino-Soviet split up to 1962 for strategic reasons. During 1959–61, Mao was acutely aware of the strategic need to achieve Sino-Soviet détente in order to neutralize the main threat, the American imperialists. In managing the Sino-Soviet dispute, the Chairman was not overly stubborn and dogmatic; instead, he was pragmatic enough to make reasonable calculations of power politics.[28]

Other scholars agree that Mao saw the Sino-Soviet split as a power struggle, namely for the leadership of the international Communist movement, but that struggle was grounded in China's unique historical-cultural context. To Mao, who had experienced first hand European and Japanese imperialism, New China should never be controlled and exploited by foreign powers. While Mao had accepted China's junior status in the early 1950s, he could not accept permanent inequality in the Sino-Soviet alliance. Especially from 1956, when Khrushchev was seen as deviating from true Marxism–Leninism, Mao could no longer tolerate 'Soviet big-power chauvinism'. To Sergey Radchenko, 'the intrinsic inequality of the Sino-Soviet alliance' was at the heart of the split.[29] In this regard, according to Shu Guang Zhang, personality, feelings, and perceptions played a vital role in Mao's ever-increasing hypersensitivity to 'unequal' relations and Moscow's attempts to control China, as manifested in the 1958 Soviet proposal for a joint submarine flotilla.[30]

In short, ideological disagreement, power struggle, and Mao's sensitivity to perceived unequal relations interacted with each other, contributing to the virtual collapse of the Sino-Soviet alliance by 1964. No longer seeing the Soviet Union as a reliable ally, Mao reasserted China's identity as the leader of developing nations and of the wars of national liberation in the Third World, particularly in Vietnam.

Notes

1 Chen Jian, *Mao's China and the Cold War* (Chapel Hill: The University of North Carolina Press, 2001), 72–3.
2 Ibid., 73–5.
3 See Thomas J. Christensen, *Useful Adversaries: Grand Strategy, Domestic Mobilization, and Sino-American Conflict, 1947–1958* (Princeton: Princeton University Press, 1996), 194–241.
4 Lorenz M. Luthi, *The Sino-Soviet Split: Cold War in the Communist World* (Princeton: Princeton University Press, 2008), 80–113.
5 Ibid., 116–21.
6 Ibid., 126–35.
7 See Chen Jian, 'The Tibetan Rebellion of 1959 and China's Changing Relations with India and the Soviet Union', *JCWS* 8: 3 (Summer 2006): 54–101.
8 Chen, *Mao's China and the Cold War*, 80–2.
9 Danhui Li and Yafeng Xia, 'Competing for Leadership: Split or Détente in the Sino-Soviet Bloc, 1959–61', *IHR* 30: 3 (September 2008): 551–5.
10 Ibid., 555–8.
11 Ibid., 566–7.
12 Luthi, op. cit., 174–8.
13 Shu Guang Zhang argues that culture-bound irrational factors such as perceptions, images, and feelings were more significant than rational calculations of costs and benefits to the collapse of Sino-Soviet economic relations. See 'Sino-Soviet Economic Cooperation', in Odd Arne Westad (ed.), *Brothers in Arms: The Rise and Fall of the Sino-Soviet Alliance, 1945–1963* (Stanford: Stanford University Press, 1998), 214–17.
14 Frank Dikötter, *Mao's Great Famine: The History of China's Most Devastating Catastrophe, 1958–1962* (London: Bloomsbury, 2010), 104–7.
15 Li and Xia, op. cit., 568–9.
16 Luthi, op. cit., 182–91.
17 Ibid., 191.
18 Li Jie, 'Change in China's Domestic Situation in the 1960s and Sino-U.S. Relations', in Robert S. Ross and Jiang Changbin (eds), *Re-examining the*

Cold War: U.S.–China Diplomacy, 1954–1973 (Cambridge, Mass.: Harvard University Press, 2001), 290–9.

19 Qiang Zhai, *China and the Vietnam Wars, 1950–1975* (Chapel Hill: The University of North Carolina Press, 2000), 114–15.

20 Noam Kochavi, *A Conflict Perpetuated: China Policy during the Kennedy Years* (Westport: Praeger, 2002), 114–15.

21 John W. Garver, 'China's Decision for War with India in 1962', in Alastair Iain Johnston and Robert S. Ross (eds), *New Directions in the Study of China's Foreign Policy* (Stanford: Stanford University Press, 2006), 86–130.

22 Luthi, op. cit., 224–8, 244.

23 *Mao Zedong on Diplomacy*, 387–8.

24 John Garver, *Foreign Relations of the People's Republic of China* (Englewood Cliffs, N.J.: Prentice Hall, 1993), 141–4.

25 Xiaohong Liu, *Chinese Ambassadors: The Rise of Diplomatic Professionalism since 1949* (Hong Kong: Hong Kong University Press, 2001), 61–3. On the French perspective, see Garret Martin, 'Playing the China Card? Revisiting France's Recognition of Communist China, 1963–64', *JCWS* 10: 1 (Winter 2008): 52–80.

26 Shu Guang Zhang, 'Between "Paper" and "Real Tigers": Mao's View of Nuclear Weapons', in John Lewis Gaddis and others (eds), *Cold War Statesmen Confront the Bomb: Nuclear Diplomacy since 1945* (Oxford: Oxford University Press, 1999), 194–215.

27 Luthi, op. cit.; Chen, *Mao's China and the Cold War*.

28 Dong Wang, 'The Quarrelling Brothers: New Chinese Archives and a Reappraisal of the Sino-Soviet Split, 1959–62', *CWIHPWP* 49 (2006).

29 Sergey Radchenko, *Two Suns in the Heavens: The Sino-Soviet Struggle for Supremacy, 1962–1967* (Stanford: Stanford University Press, 2009), 206.

30 Zhang, op. cit.

5 The Vietnam War and Cultural Revolution diplomacy, 1965–8

In the course of the 'long 1964', the Lyndon Johnson administration gradually escalated the war in Vietnam, which culminated in the July 1965 decision to commit American ground troops to South Vietnam. In response to the US escalation, China increased its military and economic assistance to North Vietnam and the National Liberation Front (NLF) in the South. After Mao unleashed the Great Proletarian Cultural Revolution in 1966, China found itself confronting not only the United States and the Soviet Union but almost all members of the world community.

China's support for North Vietnam

Notwithstanding the 1954 Geneva Agreement, the United States and South Vietnam, fearful of a possible Communist victory, blocked the holding of a nationwide plebiscite on the unification of Vietnam in 1956. The US administration propped up the inefficient and increasingly unpopular South Vietnamese regime under Ngo Dinh Diem through nation-building programmes and the dispatch of American 'advisors'. But by mid-1963, anti-government sentiment and activities in South Vietnam had reached such a level that Washington came to see Diem as more a liability than an asset. In early November, Diem was assassinated in a coup led by disgruntled South Vietnamese generals with Washington's acquiescence. The assassination of Diem encouraged North Vietnam to adopt, in December, an offensive strategy of intensifying its military assistance to the NLF in the South.

The situation deteriorated further as a result of the Gulf of Tonkin Incident in 1964. On 2 August, North Vietnamese patrol boats fired on US destroyers in the Gulf of Tonkin. Two days later, a second attack was allegedly reported by the Americans. We now know that the first assault was ordered by a local North Vietnamese commander, while the second incident did not even occur. Nonetheless, the Johnson administration responded to the events by first ordering air strikes against North Vietnamese installations and then obtaining from the US Congress the Gulf of Tonkin Resolution, which authorized the President to use military forces to protect American interests in Southeast Asia if necessary. In 1965 Johnson, having won his own mandate in the November presidential election, escalated the war. In retaliation for Viet Cong attacks on the US barracks at Pleiku, in early February he ordered US air strikes on North Vietnamese military installations. In early March, the United States launched continuous air bombing against North Vietnam codenamed Operation Rolling Thunder, and sent 3,500 marines to Danang Bay in the South. The next month, Johnson ordered the dispatch of another two divisions. The defining moment of US escalation came on 28 July, when Johnson announced the commitment of an additional 100,000 troops to South Vietnam.

The Gulf of Tonkin Incident and the bombing of North Vietnam came as a surprise to China, which had not predicted such a level of American involvement. Back in mid-1962, during Ho Chi Minh's visit to Beijing, the Chinese leaders had agreed to supply 90,000 rifles and guns for equipping up to 230 Vietnamese infantry battalions. During his official visit to Hanoi in May 1963, Liu Shaoqi had assured Ho of unswerving Chinese support for the North Vietnamese struggle. As the Americans escalated the Vietnam conflict, in April 1965 Beijing and Hanoi entered into formal agreement on the dispatch of Chinese anti-aircraft troops and logistic units to North Vietnam.[1]

In supporting North Vietnam, China was motivated by a mix of security and ideological considerations. Mao saw the escalation of the Vietnam War as part of Washington's intensified efforts to encircle the PRC. As the Chairman spoke of the American threat to China's national security in March 1965: 'The hands of the Americans stretch very far, committing aggression everywhere … American troops are now occupying our Taiwan, South Korea and many places in Japan, as well as waging war in Vietnam.'[2] The intrusion of US aircraft into China's airspace over Hainan Island on 8–9 April confirmed Mao's apprehensions about US aggressiveness.

Mao's growing sense of insecurity was manifested in the decision to launch the 'Third Front Defence' project in 1964. The project centred on the relocation of strategically important yet vulnerable industries and cities, primarily in the coastal provinces, to the remote western and south-western provinces of China. It involved heavy financial commitment at both the central and provincial levels and the construction of completely new cities in China's mountainous interior. The aim was to create a massive, self-sufficient strategic base area to meet the contingency of war with the United States. On 10 August 1964, after the Gulf of Tonkin Incident, Mao ordered the gradual implementation of the Third Front project.[3]

Ideologically, Mao was aware of the significant ramifications of the North Vietnamese struggle for both the global wars of national liberation and China's domestic politics. With the virtual collapse of the Sino-Soviet alliance and the American involvement in Vietnam in 1964–5, Mao attached great importance to the revolutionary struggles in the Afro-Asian-Latin American 'intermediate zone', centred on China. In Asia he saw Vietnam as the most serious victim of US aggression and the most essential test case of China's leadership in the international liberation movements. Mao firmly believed that the Chinese revolutionary model of 'people's war' best suited the particular circumstances of Vietnam and the Third World generally. His thinking was enunciated in an article entitled 'Long Live the Victory of People's War' published in Defence Minister Lin Biao's name on 2 September 1965. In commemoration of the twentieth anniversary of the Chinese victory in the War of Resistance against Japan, the article underscored Mao's successful strategy and tactics of 'people's war' – guerrilla warfare in the countryside, mass mobilization, and the policy of 'self-reliance'. In the circumstances of the mid-1960s, the article called for the Asian, African, and Latin American nations, or 'the rural areas of the world', to encircle and eventually defeat 'the cities of the world' represented by North America and Western Europe through 'people's wars'. It must be added that Lin's piece was directed as much against the Soviet revisionists as against the American imperialists. By criticizing the Khrushchev revisionists for having 'no faith in the masses' and for being 'afraid of U.S. imperialism, of war and of revolution', Lin and Mao conveyed the message that the Third World countries should look to China, not the Soviet Union, for inspiration and leadership in their revolutionary struggles.[4]

Mao, moreover, saw China's involvement in Vietnam as a way to discredit the 'revisionists' at home. In the mid-1960s, the Chairman felt increasingly uneasy about the pragmatic economic policies pursued by Liu and Deng and the role of the Party apparatus in Chinese politics generally. Mao feared that the 'revisionist' tendencies, if unchecked, would result in the 'restoration of capitalism' in China. The US escalation of the Vietnam War added to Mao's fears of possible collusion between domestic and external enemies. By committing China to Hanoi's national liberation struggle, Mao hoped to mobilize the Chinese population against all revisionists, imperialists, and reactionaries.[5]

While Mao was determined to render support to North Vietnam, he was anxious to avoid a Korean War-type confrontation with the United States. The Korean War experience reminded Mao of the danger of mutual misperceptions in crisis: in September 1950 Zhou had warned Washington, via the Indian Ambassador, that the US crossing of the thirty-eighth parallel would lead to Chinese intervention, but unfortunately the warning was ignored. In 1965 Mao was eager to ensure that the Johnson administration would not misinterpret his desire to avoid a direct Sino-American confrontation over Vietnam. This time, China relied on Pakistan, a US ally. At first, President Ayub Khan was asked to deliver the Chinese message to Johnson during his forthcoming visit to Washington in April. But the sudden American cancellation of Khan's visit caused Beijing to explore other channels of communication. The Chinese turned to the British. During his meeting with the British Chargé d'Affaires in Beijing on 31 May, Foreign Minister Chen Yi stated firmly that, although China would 'not provoke war with the United States', it was 'prepared for war'. If America attacked China or directly invaded North Vietnam, Chen said, 'that would mean war and there would be no limits to the war'. And 'what China says counts'. The Americans did not miss the Chinese warning this time around. In June, Chen's four-point message was considered by State Department officials including Secretary of State Dean Rusk and brought to the attention of Johnson. Consequently, both America and China understood the scope and limits of the other side's involvement in the Vietnam War.[6]

Between 1965 and 1969, China provided massive economic and military assistance to North Vietnam in three main areas. First, Chinese engineering troops were dispatched to help construct and maintain defence works, airfields, roads, and railways in North Vietnam. Second, Beijing sent a total of 16 divisions of Chinese anti-aircraft artillery units to North Vietnam, whose primary tasks were to defend strategically significant targets such as the railway lines linking Hanoi and other places, and to protect the Chinese engineering troops. Although the Chinese anti-aircraft units did not engage in operations south of Hanoi, and the Chinese air force was never directly involved in operations over Vietnamese territory, their presence allowed the North Vietnamese to infiltrate their own forces into the South and fight the Americans. Finally, China supplied North Vietnam and the NLF with massive amounts of military equipment including guns, ammunition, radio transmitters, tanks, ships, and uniforms. All in all, with over 320,000 Chinese engineering and anti-aircraft forces present on North Vietnamese soil from 1965 through 1969, China played a major, if indirect, role in the Vietnam War, deterring a possible American ground invasion of the North.[7]

Sino-Soviet conflict over Vietnam

China's relations with the Soviet Union deteriorated further during the Vietnam War. Vietnam sharpened the Sino-Soviet competition for influence in the Third World. To Moscow, Mao not only had challenged the Soviet leading position in Eastern Europe but now also exploited the Chinese model of a 'people's war' to undermine Soviet influence in the Third World.[8] After Khrushchev's downfall in October 1964, First Secretary Leonid Brezhnev adopted a more proactive policy regarding the Vietnam War. In February 1965, Moscow began to provide military and economic aid to North Vietnam, which had hitherto looked to Beijing alone for supplies.

In February 1965 the Soviet Prime Minister, Aleksei Kosygin, asked Zhou Enlai to allow the speedy delivery of Soviet anti-aircraft armament to Hanoi by air in view of the intensifying US bombing raids. But suspicious of the Soviet real motives, Zhou insisted on arms being transported by railway. (Not until early 1966 did Beijing agree to selected air transports.) The same month, the Soviets also requested the use of two airfields near Kunming in southern China for the stationing of MIG-21 fighters together with 500 Soviet personnel as well as Beijing's agreement to the transport of 4,000 Soviet anti-aircraft missile troops to Vietnam through China. Worried that Hanoi would become too dependent on Moscow's support especially for advanced weaponry which China lacked, Beijing turned down the Soviet requests. Disputes over the delivery of Soviet military aid via China continued throughout the subsequent years, with Moscow accusing Beijing of deliberate obstructionism. It appeared, though, that logistical difficulties such as the bottlenecks in the Vietnamese railway system and the inefficiencies of the Soviet bureaucracy were probably the real causes of delivery problems between 1965 and 1969.[9]

Beijing and Moscow also differed over peace negotiations with the Americans. While rendering military and economic aid to Hanoi, the Soviets did not rule out the possibility of a negotiated settlement in Vietnam. In February 1965, during his visits to Hanoi and Beijing, Kosygin proposed the convening of an international conference on Indochina similar to the 1954 Geneva Conference where the Soviet Union was a co-chair. Other countries such as India, Ghana, and France also endeavoured to a find a peaceful solution through their own initiatives. Nonetheless, until 1969 China vehemently opposed any peace talks between Hanoi and Washington. Confident of the ultimate success of the 'people's war' in Vietnam and eager to mobilize the Chinese population for ideological purposes, Mao insisted that the United States be expelled from Indochina through armed struggles. Besides, Mao was fearful of Soviet–American collusion at Vietnam's expense, and did not hesitate to accuse Moscow of selling out to Hanoi in the pursuit of détente with Washington.[10]

In the mid-1960s, Mao had to struggle not only with the Soviet revisionists but also with the 'revisionists' at home such as Liu Shaoqi and Peng Zhen, the mayor of Beijing. In 1966 he unleashed the Cultural Revolution.

Cultural revolution in the Chinese foreign ministry

The Cultural Revolution was an intensely ideological and political movement launched by Mao and participated in by millions of Chinese people, especially the Chinese youth or the 'Red Guards', to rid China of corrupt bureaucrats, 'capitalist-roaders', and 'revisionists'. It seriously affected China's foreign policy and external relations. In August 1966, on Mao's instructions, the Eleventh Plenum of the CCP Central Committee removed Liu Shaoqi and Deng Xiaoping from power, thus causing the complete paralysis of the Politburo and the Central Secretariat (which had hitherto been handled on a daily basis by the two leaders respectively). With Mao's patronage, the Central Cultural Revolution Group (CCRG), comprising radicals such as Mao's wife Jiang Qing, the writer Yao Wengyuan, and the security chief Kang Sheng, emerged to fill the political void. After the February Adverse Current in February 1967, in which most of the Politburo members came under attack, Mao decided that the CCRG should act as the main body of decision-making, both domestic and foreign. This arrangement allowed the CCRG to interfere with foreign affairs, and the current of 'ultra-leftism' descended over the Ministry of Foreign Affairs (MFA).

At the opening stage of the Cultural Revolution in 1966, Foreign Minister Chen Yi had supported the sending of 'work teams' to the MFA. But after the beginning of 'power seizure' in 1967, Chen became the main target of attack by radical rebel organizations, which were entrusted with 'supervising' the Ministry's work. Although protected by the pragmatic Zhou Enlai, who sought to ensure his own political survival by both encouraging and restraining the Cultural Revolution within the MFA, Chen was forced to make self-criticism on a number of occasions. The MFA vice-ministers were not exempt from radical rebels' assaults: Zhang Hanfu, Ji Pengfei, and Qiao Guanhua were forced to abandon their duties and to reflect on their 'bourgeois' thinking and lifestyle.[11]

The climax of the Cultural Revolution within the MFA came in August. On 7 August, Wang Li, a senior member of the CCRG, delivered a speech to Yao Dengshan (the former Chinese Chargé d'Affaires in Indonesia who had been expelled by the host government and was given the title 'red diplomatic soldier' upon his return to China) and representatives of radical rebel organizations, calling for thorough 'power seizure' in the MFA. Emboldened by Wang's talk, on 19 August, the MFA radical rebels in cooperation with the Red Guards from Beijing's Foreign Languages Institute seized power in the Department of Political Affairs of the Ministry. In the following few days, the Red Guards chanted 'Down with Chen Yi', and his possible replacement by Yao Dengshan, and the vice-ministers were forced to write self-criticism in the basement of the MFA building. The MFA, according to Zhou, was completely out of control for four days. It was during this period, on 22 August, that one of the most serious incidents of China's foreign relations during the Cultural Revolution took place – the sacking of the British Embassy in Beijing.[12]

Proletarian diplomacy of the 'revolutionary masses'

During the radical phase of the Cultural Revolution (1966–9), China 'held high the banner of anti-imperialism and anti-revisionism', taking on not only the two superpowers but indeed the whole world. Mao imposed self-isolation on China by recalling all its overseas ambassadors to participate in the Cultural Revolution at home, except for Huang Hua of Egypt. Between mid-1966 and 1967, China had disputes with over 30 of the 50 countries with which it had diplomatic relations. While the CCRG played a role in the growth of ultra-leftism within the MFA, it was the 'revolutionary masses' – overseas Chinese students and workers, low-ranking Chinese Embassy staff who stayed behind, and radical Red Guards in China – that actually meddled in foreign affairs through 'proletarian diplomacy'.[13] By zealously propagating Mao Zedong's thought, distributing the *Quotations of Chairman Mao* (or 'the little red book'), and staging anti-foreign demonstrations, the 'proletarian diplomatic fighters' on their own created ugly incidents with foreigners and foreign governments particularly during the turbulent year of 1967.

The Soviet revisionists stood out as one of the main targets of the 'revolutionary masses'. Long before the onset of the Cultural Revolution, on 4 March 1965 approximately 2,000 East Asian students, many of whom were Chinese, had attacked the US Embassy in Moscow. According to Lorenz Luthi, the attack, presumably encouraged and supported by Beijing, was aimed as much to embarrass the Soviets as to provoke the Americans in the light of the US escalation of the Vietnam War and the growing Sino-Soviet conflict over Vietnam.[14] In August 1966, after the Cultural Revolution started, the Red Guards began days-long demonstrations in front of the Soviet Embassy in Beijing, putting up 'big character posters' (*dazibao*) on the walls of the embassy buildings and renaming the street where they were located 'Anti-Revisionism Street'.[15]

As the 'seizure of power' campaign swept China in early 1967, more anti-Soviet incidents ensued. On 25 January, 69 Chinese students from Europe stopped in Moscow on their way back to China. They proceeded to the Lenin Mausoleum in Red Square and publicly read Mao's quotations, provoking brutal suppression by the Soviet police. The Chinese Embassy in Moscow lodged a strongly worded protest with the Soviet Foreign Ministry. On the other hand, the Soviet Embassy in Beijing was bombarded by Red Guards' demonstrations and loudspeaker propaganda for days. On 11 February a mass rally, attended by Zhou, Chen Boda, and other leaders, was held in Beijing, condemning the Soviet revisionists. Similar anti-Soviet demonstrations occurred in other provinces. The violent demonstrations set alarm bells ringing through the Kremlin, raising the prospect of war with China.[16]

But the defining incidents of China's proletarian diplomacy were the so-called 'three smashes and one burn' – the attacks on the Indonesian, Indian, and Burmese embassies and the burning of the office of the British Chargé d'Affaires in China. On some occasions, the Chinese reacted, if over-zealously, to foreign provocations rather than instigated the incidents in the first place. Sino-Indonesian relations had been deteriorating rapidly since 1965, following the abortive 30 September coup by young radical officers supported by the Indonesian Communist Party (PKI) and the resulting toppling of pro-Beijing Sukarno by General Suharto. Consequently, the Chinese Embassy in Jakarta, suspected of supporting the PKI, was attacked by the Indonesians; so was the economically dominant ethnic Chinese community. With the violence of the Cultural Revolution, the relationship had become so sour that on 24 April 1967 the Indonesian government declared Chinese Chargé d'Affaires Yao Dengshan and Consul General Xu Ren *personae non gratae* and ordered them to leave the country. The Chinese authorities retaliated by expelling the Indonesian Chargé d'Affaires in Beijing, and organized a huge demonstration in front of the Indonesian Embassy, during which the 'revolutionary masses' forced their way into the embassy building. In August the Red Guards stormed the Indonesian Embassy in response to the attacks on the Chinese Embassy in Indonesia. In October, Indonesia severed diplomatic relations with China, and the two countries closed down their respective embassies.[17]

The Indian example underscored Beijing's violation of the Western concept of diplomatic immunity from jurisdiction. According to the 1961 Vienna Convention on Diplomatic Relations, diplomats were exempted from trial by the courts of the state to which they were accredited. But the PRC did not feel bound by the diplomatic norms of the international community which it maintained were shaped by the Western capitalist powers. On 12 June 1967, the MFA informed the Indian Embassy in Beijing that the Chinese government no longer recognized the diplomatic status of M. K. Raghunath, the Embassy's second secretary, and that he was not permitted to leave China until the completion of the judicial process regarding his 'crimes'. Raghunath was accused of 'espionage', collecting political and military intelligence on China and taking photos in a prohibited military zone. A few days later, a special tribunal tried Raghunath in his absence in the Workers' Stadium and sentenced the accused to immediate expulsion. Raghunath was escorted to Beijing Airport for a flight to Hong Kong, after being beaten and humiliated by the Red Guards.[18] While the poor state of Sino-Indian relations was the underlying cause, the Raghunath spy case demonstrated the Chinese paranoia about foreigners under the climate of ultra-leftism.[19]

Even friendly countries such as Burma could not escape dispute with China. The problem started with Chinese students in Burma propagating Mao's ideas and wearing Mao badges to classes. In late June the Burmese government took steps to suppress the Chinese students' activities. The Chinese schools and the Chinese Embassy in Rangoon came under attack by local mobs, during which a dozen Chinese were killed. In response, the MFA protested in the strongest terms possible to the Burmese government, and as many as 1 million Chinese people laid siege to the Burmese Embassy in Beijing for four consecutive days. Anti-Chinese protests, in turn, erupted in several Burmese cities. The cycle of attacks and counter-attacks brought Sino-Burmese relations to a new low.[20]

The dismissal of the British Chargé d'Affaires in late August was the most serious of all Chinese attacks on foreign embassies but also the turning point in the proletarian diplomacy of the Red Guards. The attack was inextricably linked with the disturbance in Hong Kong, which was in turn a political spillover of the Cultural Revolution. In May 1967 an industrial dispute in Hong Kong triggered a territory-wide anti-colonial struggle by the left-wing elements, characterized by strikes, border clashes, and bombing campaigns. The colonial authorities adopted a hard-line approach to restoring law and order. From the outset, Beijing supported the 'Maoists' in Hong Kong. While Zhou Enlai argued that the 'Cultural Revolution-style' struggle was not for export to Hong Kong, the MFA lodged diplomatic protests with the British government and endorsed Red Guard demonstrations in support of the Hong Kong struggle. In July the Hong Kong authorities arrested a news worker of the local New China News Agency – the *de facto* Chinese Embassy – and later sentenced him to two years' imprisonment. Beijing retaliated with the house arrest of the British correspondent of Reuters in China, Anthony Grey. In response to Hong Kong's suspension of three left-wing newspapers and arrest of more left-wing journalists, on 20 August the MFA issued a note to the British government, calling for the lifting of the suspension and the release of all 'patriotic journalists' within 48 hours, otherwise Britain would face 'consequences'.

On the night of 22 August, the 'revolutionary masses', mainly Red Guards from the Institute of Foreign Languages and other universities in Beijing, demonstrated in front of the office of the British Chargé d'Affaires. Shortly after the expiry of the '48-hour ultimatum', the Red Guards attacked the office, notwithstanding Zhou's last-minute calls for restraint. In the process, the office building was largely gutted by fire, and the Chargé d'Affaire's house was ransacked. The 23 hostages (diplomats and their wives), having suffered humiliation and harassment at the hands of the radical mobs, eventually escaped to safety without serious injuries, thanks to the involvement of the Beijing Garrison Command under Zhou's orders.[21]

The manner in which the British office was attacked and destroyed shocked Zhou and even Mao. Upon receiving the news, on the early morning of 23 August, Zhou called an emergency meeting with the representatives of the MFA, the Beijing Garrison Command, and the rebel organizations, criticizing the burning of the British office. Later, Zhou attributed the sacking to the influence of ultra-leftism and 'anarchism' within the MFA in August, while excusing himself for sanctioning the 20 August ultimatum due to tiredness. Mao also distanced himself from the excesses of the Red Guards and radical rebels by conveniently scapegoating Wang Li and Yao Dengshan, both of whom were subsequently purged by the Party.[22]

After all the attacks on foreign embassies in the summer of 1967, Mao and Zhou were anxious to restore normality to the MFA and China's diplomacy generally. In March 1968, Zhou admitted to the CCRG and MFA staff that: 'we are now isolated. No one wants to make friends with us.' In May, Mao ordered that the use of the slogan 'Beijing as the centre of the world revolution' in propaganda should be stopped.[23] There were twists and turns in China's foreign policy, though, due to the ongoing power struggle between the 'moderates' (represented by Zhou) and the 'radicals' (represented by Jiang Qing and Lin Biao). Sino-British relations, for instance, remained unstable as a result of the 'hostage crisis'. Following the sacking of the British office, the British diplomats in China, together with Grey and other British residents, were held as *de facto* hostages by the Communist authorities as bargaining chips for the release of Hong Kong's left-wing prisoners relating to the 1967 riots.[24]

Nonetheless, by the summer of 1968, Mao no longer encouraged and endorsed the kind of proletarian diplomacy that had caused so much damage to China's international reputation a year earlier. He deployed the PLA to restore order across the country and dissolved the Red Guards by sending them to the countryside for re-education. More significantly, Mao came to realize that China's main enemy was not India, Indonesia, or Britain but the Soviet Union. Following the Tet Offensive and the opening of the Paris peace talks, both of which Beijing opposed, North Vietnam drifted towards Moscow's position on the Vietnam War. In August, the Soviet Union invaded Czechoslovakia to suppress the 'counter-revolutionary forces' and proclaimed the Brezhnev doctrine of 'limited sovereignty'. Together with increased Sino-Soviet border clashes, China turned its attention to its northern neighbour.

Revolutionary power or status-quo power?

How 'revolutionary' was China's foreign policy at the height of the Vietnam War and the Cultural Revolution? At first glance, China appeared to be a revolutionary power, supporting the Communist revolution in Vietnam, confronting simultaneously the two superpowers, and challenging the diplomatic norms of the international community. The launching of the Cultural Revolution represented Mao's efforts to carry his 'continuous revolution' to the highest stage. China became more critical than ever in defining friends and enemies in accordance with Maoism, taking on not only old enemies such as the Soviet Union and India but also hitherto friendly Asian and African countries such as Burma and Kenya. All ambassadors except one were recalled to the mainland to join the revolution. In brief, Mao chose to isolate China from the world for the sake of revolutionary purity.

Nevertheless, as Odd Arne Westad puts it: 'The PRC's foreign policy in the mid-1960s was … high on rhetoric but low on action. [With the exception of Vietnam,] China's general direction during the Great Proletarian Cultural Revolution was inward and away from engaging foreign revolutions.'[25] Melvin Gurtov also argues that 'the nature of the [Cultural] Revolution, as well as events since the autumn of 1967, indicate no real revolution in foreign policy'. The Cultural Revolution was primarily 'an internal phenomenon' and 'did not bring with it military adventures' abroad.[26] Besides, China's self-imposed isolation was short-lived. As early as the autumn of 1967, Mao saw the imperative need to curb the influence of ultra-leftism in China's foreign policy. During the Cultural Revolution, the MFA did not suffer the same degree of factionalism and disruption as other ministries due to the importance Mao and Zhou attached to foreign affairs.[27]

In fact, the ritual violence against the foreign embassies in China during 1967 was largely the spontaneous initiatives of the 'revolutionary masses', which were more 'Maoist' than Mao himself: they wanted to prove their revolutionary credentials and to impress the Chairman. Likewise, the 'proletarian diplomatic fighters' abroad zealously disseminated Mao Zedong's thoughts and in the process brought themselves into confrontation with the host government and local people. Preoccupied with the domestic power struggles, Mao, Zhou, and the MFA more often reacted to the proletarian diplomacy of the Red Guards, and capitalized on the anti-foreign incidents, once they had been provoked, through moral endorsement. But when the Red Guards were perceived to have gone too far, Mao, for all his revolutionary rhetoric, was pragmatic enough to exercise a moderate influence on the conduct of China's foreign policy. Peter Van Ness contends that it was 'unlikely' that 'Mao has purposefully sought to create diplomatic incidents and make enemies of most of the more important governments of the world'. While some attacks, such as the one on the Soviet Union, might have been 'intentional', other incidents 'have resulted from what seem to be unintended, but perhaps unavoidable, effects of the Cultural Revolution on Chinese foreign affairs'.[28]

In the mid-1960s, China was a 'radical nationalist state', being 'predominantly socialistic at home and nationalistic in foreign affairs'.[29] After 1968, the 'nationalistic' or 'pragmatic' component of China's identity became even more prominent, as Mao had to deal with the intensified Soviet threat.

Notes

1 See Qiang Zhai, *China and the Vietnam Wars, 1950–1975* (Chapel Hill: The University of North Carolina Press, 2000), 112–56.

2 *Mao Zedong on Diplomacy*, 429–30.
3 See Lorenz Luthi, 'The Vietnam War and China's Third-Line Defense Planning before the Cultural Revolution, 1964–66', *JCWS* 10: 1 (Winter 2008): 26–51.
4 William E. Griffith, *Sino-Soviet Relations, 1964–1965* (Cambridge, Mass.: The MIT Press, 1967), 424–42.
5 Chen Jian, *Mao's China and the Cold War* (Chapel Hill: The University of North Carolina Press, 2001), 209–11.
6 James G. Hershberg and Chen Jian, 'Reading and Warning the Likely Enemy: China's Signals to the United States about Vietnam', *IHR* 27: 1 (March 2005): 47–84.
7 Chen, op. cit., 221–9.
8 Odd Arne Westad, *The Global Cold War: Third World Interventions and the Making of Our Times* (Cambridge: Cambridge University Press, 2005), 160–70.
9 Li Danhui, 'The Sino-Soviet Dispute over Assistance for Vietnam's Anti-American War, 1965–72', in Priscilla Roberts (ed.), *Behind the Bamboo Curtain: China, Vietnam, and the World beyond Asia* (Stanford: Stanford University Press, 2006), 289–304, 311–13.
10 Zhai, op. cit., 157–68.
11 Barbara Barnouin and Yu Changgen, *Chinese Foreign Policy During the Cultural Revolution* (London: Kegan Paul International, 1998), 57–61.
12 Xiaohong Liu, *Chinese Ambassadors: The Rise of Diplomatic Professionalism since 1949* (Hong Kong: Hong Kong University Press, 2001), 114–15.
13 I borrowed the term from Lorenz M. Luthi, 'The Origins of Proletarian Diplomacy: The Chinese Attack on the American Embassy in the Soviet Union, 4 March 1965', *CWH* 9: 3 (August 2009): 411–26.
14 See ibid.
15 Sergey Radchenko, *Two Suns in the Heavens: The Sino-Soviet Struggle for Supremacy, 1962–1967* (Stanford: Stanford University Press, 2009), 178–80.
16 Ibid., 188–93.
17 Ma Jisen, *The Cultural Revolution in the Foreign Ministry of China* (Hong Kong: The Chinese University Press, 2004), 165–7.
18 Philippe Ardant, 'Chinese Diplomatic Practice during the Cultural Revolution', in Jerome Alan Cohen (ed.), *China's Practice of International Law: Some Case Studies* (Cambridge, Mass.: Harvard University Press, 1972), 99–102.
19 Anne-Marie Brady, *Making the Foreign Serve China: Managing Foreigners in the People's Republic* (Lanham: Rowman & Littlefield, 2003), 164–5.
20 Barnouin and Yu, op. cit., 74–5.
21 Ma, op. cit., 178–88.
22 Ibid., 205–6; Barnouin and Yu, op. cit., 27–9.
23 Gong Li, 'China Decision Making and the Thawing of U.S.–China Relations', in Robert S. Ross and Jiang Changbin (eds), *Re-examining the Cold War: U.S.–China Diplomacy, 1954–1973* (Cambridge, Mass.: Harvard University Press, 2001), 323.
24 See Chi-kwan Mark, 'Hostage Diplomacy: Britain, China, and the Politics of Negotiation, 1967–69', *Diplomacy & Statecraft* 20: 3 (September 2009): 473–93.
25 Westad, op. cit., 184.
26 Melvin Gurtov, 'The Foreign Ministry and Foreign Affairs during the Cultural Revolution', *CQ* 40 (October–December 1969): 102.

27 Lu Ning, *The Dynamics of Foreign Policy Decisionmaking in China* (Boulder: Westview Press, 1997), 59.
28 Peter Van Ness, *Revolution and Chinese Foreign Policy: Peking's Support for Wars of National Liberation* (Berkeley: University of California Press, 1970), 237.
29 Ibid., 196.

6   Sino-Soviet Border War and Sino-American Rapprochement, 1969–72

By 1969 the radical phase of the Cultural Revolution was over, but not the movement itself. The CCP's Ninth Congress, held on 1–24 April, marked the beginning of the end of the Cultural Revolution, albeit in a painfully slow manner. It approved the revised Party constitution and elected a new Central Committee and Politburo. The CCRG gradually ceased to function, and decision-making power was restored to the Politburo. Nonetheless, the influence of radicalism did not dissipate with the CCRG. Indeed, the new Politburo included not only pragmatic members such as Zhou Enlai but also Jiang Qing and her allies, or the 'Gang of Four', and Lin Biao, Mao's designated successor. Thus, policy-making continued to be complicated by the power struggle between the 'pragmatists' and the 'radicals' (which were divided into Jiang's and Lin's cliques), with Mao playing one group off against the other and making the final decision.[1]

The year 1969 also saw the beginning of the end of China's image as an international outcast. Slowly but surely, ambassadors were re-sent to overseas postings to resume normal diplomatic functions. By late 1971 the PRC was voted into the UN by an overwhelming majority. But the most significant development in China's foreign relations during 1969–72 was Mao's redefinition of China's identity as America's 'friend' against its new principal enemy, the Soviet Union.

Sino-Soviet Border War

Sino-Soviet relations after the downfall of Khrushchev in late 1964 saw no signs of significant improvement, for Mao characterized Soviet policy as 'Khrushchevism without Khrushchev'. Indeed, the Sino-Soviet dispute was militarized: both countries increased the number of troops along their border, and Moscow concluded a defence treaty with Outer Mongolia in 1966. Between October 1964 and March 1969, according to Beijing, the number of incidents was over 4,000, focusing on the eastern side of the border particularly the Zhenbao and Qiliqin Islands on the Wusuli (Ussuri) River. After the Soviet invasion of Czechoslovakia in late 1968, the situation along the Sino-Soviet border deteriorated rapidly. Violent incidents on Zhenbao Island started on 27 December, and at least six more clashes occurred through early 1969. On 2 March, the Soviet and Chinese border garrisons on Zhenbao Island engaged in a major armed conflict, and two weeks later, on 15 March, an even fiercer clash erupted. The clashes marked the onset of the 1969 Sino-Soviet Border War.

According to Yang Kuisong,[2] Mao had planned the military confrontation in order to achieve broader strategic objectives. Through a major but limited armed operation, Mao wanted to teach the Soviets 'a bitter lesson' for the escalating border clashes since late 1968. The Chairman also hoped to exploit a supposedly manageable external crisis to achieve the goal of domestic mobilization. As he was winding down the Cultural Revolution in early 1969, Mao, worrying that the Chinese people would lose enthusiasm for his 'continuous revolution', wanted to use a limited military conflict to keep the nation on a high state of alert to Soviet-style 'revisionism'. An attack on Zhenbao Island in the vulnerable Russian Far East made military sense since China enjoyed the local advantage of much shorter, interior lines of supply.[3]

But Mao had overestimated his ability to control external events. On 13 August, after a series of probing attacks, the Soviets launched a major retaliatory strike on the western side of the Sino-Soviet border, close to China's Xinjiang, inflicting fatal losses on the Chinese border garrisons. Moscow apparently wanted to escalate the border war. On 18 August, a Soviet embassy official sounded out a US State Department official about possible American support for a Soviet attack on Chinese nuclear facilities. The Chinese got wind of the Soviet consideration of a pre-emptive strike later that month, when Moscow made similar enquiries of its Eastern European allies.

The Soviet escalation resulted in a war scare in Beijing. Prior to the Zhenbao attacks, in February Mao had asked the four marshals – Chen Yi, Ye Jianying, Xu Xiangqian, and Nie Rongzhen – to 'pay attention to' the international situation. After the March clashes, the four marshals produced a comprehensive report on 11 July. They concluded that it was unlikely that the United States and the Soviet Union, either jointly or separately, would launch a large-scale war against China in the foreseeable future. But after the Soviets launched the August attacks and explored the possibility of a nuclear strike, a shocked Mao immediately issued an order for war preparations. As the second phase of the 'Third Front Defence' project that had started in 1964, the Chinese government organized a large-scale evacuation of the population and main industries from the big cities, constructed air-raid underground shelters, and stockpiled daily necessities to meet the contingency of a nuclear war.

While China was making war preparations, on 6 September Soviet Premier Aleksei Kosygin suggested the holding of talks with his Chinese counterpart via the Vietnamese on the occasion of attending Ho Chi Minh's funeral in Hanoi. Suspicious of the real Soviet motives, Mao deliberated for several days before sanctioning an informal meeting between the two premiers at Beijing Airport. The meeting took place on the 11th, when Zhou and Kosygin scotched the rumour of a Soviet nuclear strike on China and each agreed to return their ambassadors to the other's capital and restore regular rail and air links. A week later, on 18 September, Zhou wrote a letter to Kosygin, confirming that both sides would relax tension by not using armed forces, including nuclear ones, against the other.

But Mao and Lin remained highly sceptical about the sudden change of heart on the Soviet part. In three Politburo meetings within a week in mid-September, the majority of the members concluded that Moscow's peace gesture was a smoke-screen designed to cover the objective of a sudden Soviet attack on China. (The memory of Japan's peace talks with Washington on the eve of the Pearl Harbor attack was invoked to support the conclusion.) It was believed that the visit to China of a Soviet delegation for border talks, scheduled for 20 October, would be the signal for launching a surprise attack on China. To meet this contingency, Mao decided that all Party, government, and military leaders should evacuate Beijing before that date: the Chairman himself would set off for Wuhan, Lin Biao would go to Suzhou, and Zhou and other key leaders, although staying in Beijing, would retreat to the underground command centre in the city's western suburbs. Sensing the urgency of a Soviet surprise attack, Lin, having arrived in Suzhou, issued on 17 October a 'Number One Order' (via his Chief of Staff), calling for the Chinese army, naval, and air forces to get into combat positions. Lin's order, however, had not been cleared by Mao, who angrily asked for it to be rescinded. (Mao's angry response was probably related to the manner in which Lin's order was issued without his prior authorization rather than the content itself.)[4]

But the expected Soviet attack did not materialize. One of the main factors was the lack of American support for a pre-emptive nuclear strike. Not only did President Richard Nixon decline joint military action, but he was anxious to prevent the impression of US–Soviet collusion against China.

Sino-American signalling for rapprochement

Nixon entered the White House at a time when American power and influence in the world was significantly weakened by the Vietnam War and the economic resurgence of West Germany and Japan. He aimed to restore America's position in a multipolar international order by pursuing détente with the Soviet Union, seeking an 'honourable peace' in Vietnam, and achieving rapprochement with Communist China. In carrying out his China initiative, Nixon relied on Henry Kissinger, National Security Advisor, not because of close personal bonds but for the latter's diplomatic skills and expertise. Obsessed with *realpolitik* and the 'strategic triangle', Kissinger approached China – indeed all countries – primarily through the lens of US–Soviet relations. By normalizing relations with China, or playing the 'China card', he hoped to exert pressure on Moscow concerning European matters. Likewise, Kissinger played the 'Soviet card' to make China more eager to cooperate with America against the perceived Soviet threat. Kissinger's personality and working style were characterized by secrecy: he disliked the State Department's involvement in China policy and instead relied on back-channel diplomacy.[5]

But the main challenge for Nixon and Kissinger was how to change China's perception of America as a principal Cold War adversary. There was no formal channel of communication between the two governments. In mid-February, Beijing had cancelled the scheduled Sino-American ambassadorial talks, suspended since early 1968, as a result of Washington's refusal to return a defected Chinese embassy official. Nixon needed to convey to Beijing the US desire for a new relationship. On 21 July the State Department announced the partial relaxation of travel and trade, allowing American citizens to visit the PRC and bring back US$100 worth of Chinese goods. During his around-the-world trip in late July and early August, Nixon told Asian leaders that America was interested in reconciliation with China. In view of the escalating Sino-Soviet border clashes, on 5 September Undersecretary of State Elliot Richardson, addressing the American Political Science Association in New York, said that the United States would not seek to exploit their hostilities, thereby hinting to Beijing that Washington would not support a Soviet nuclear strike against China.[6]

Nixon and Kissinger, however, preferred secret channels to communicate important messages to the Chinese leaders. Enjoying friendly relations with both America and China, Pakistan was seen as a reliable go-between. Having decided to terminate the US Seventh Fleet's routine patrolling in the Taiwan Strait (partly for financial reasons), Kissinger wanted to use the opportunity provided by the withdrawal of the two destroyers to impress the Chinese. In early October, Pakistani President Yahya Khan was requested to inform the Chinese of the US decision. Besides the Pakistanis, Kissinger developed Romanian and French channels to communicate secret message about the US desire for high-level talks with Beijing.

In view of the August border clashes and the ensuing war scare, Mao's attitude towards the American imperialist began to undergo subtle change. At the height of the tension, the four marshals submitted a second report on the current international situation to Mao on 17 September. Concerning the possibility of war, the report argued that the 'Soviet revisionists' fears about possible Sino-American unity makes it more difficult for them to launch an all-out attack on China'. It concluded that China 'must wage a tit-for-tat struggle against both the United States and the Soviet Union, including using negotiation as a means of fighting against them'.[7] In other words, Beijing should enter into negotiation with Washington and thus play the 'American card' against Moscow in order to prevent the latter from launching an all-out attack on China. It is not clear how Mao responded to the marshals' report at the time.[8] But the US signals of goodwill were not lost on the Chairman. Not only was he relieved to hear that the United States would not support a Soviet nuclear strike against China, but Mao also felt obliged to reciprocate the American withdrawal of the two destroyers from the Taiwan Strait by releasing, in early December, the two detained Americans whose yacht had strayed into China's territorial waters.

During 1970 Nixon and Kissinger made more overtures to China through the Pakistani and Romanian back channels. This was especially so after the United States had made an 'incursion' into Cambodia in May, an escalation that propelled China to suspend yet again the scheduled Sino-American ambassadorial talks at Warsaw, which in turn provided Kissinger with a pretext to bypass the Warsaw channel altogether. By late 1970, Mao came to realize that a rapprochement with America would be in China's interest, not only in meeting the Soviet threat but also in resolving the Taiwan question. Mao decided to send an important signal to Washington via the American journalist Edgar Snow, his old friend dating back to the Yan'an days. On the National Day of 1 October, Mao invited Snow, who was then visiting China, to review the celebration parade at the top of the Gate of

Heavenly Peace. A picture of Snow standing side by side with Mao was subsequently published on the front page of the *People's Daily*. Mao hoped to convey a message to Washington: America and China were friends just like Snow and himself. But Mao also had another audience in mind – the Chinese people. Having demonized the United States for almost two decades, Mao needed to prepare the Chinese public psychologically for seeking rapprochement with China's former adversary.[9]

Unfortunately, Washington totally missed Mao's subtle gesture. Nixon relied on the Pakistani channel instead. On 25 October he asked President Yahya Khan, who was scheduled to visit China early the next month, to pass a message about sending a high-level US emissary to Beijing. As Zhou underscored the significance of Nixon's message, 'this is the first time that the proposal has come from a Head [Nixon], through a Head [Khan], to a Head [Mao]'.[10] On 9 December, Nixon and Kissinger received a Chinese reply via Pakistani Ambassador Agha Hilaly: in view of Nixon's message, China would want to discuss 'the subject of the vacation of Chinese territories called Taiwan' and welcome a 'special envoy' of President Nixon to Beijing.

Perhaps the most dramatic signalling by Mao was China's 'ping-pong diplomacy' on the occasion of the Thirty-First World Table Tennis Championship at Nagoya, Japan, between 28 March and 7 April. To Zhou, who closely supervised the preparation of the Chinese team, the aim was friendship first and competition second. But the Chinese players were instructed not to be too proactive, for example, by talking to their American counterparts first. In the event, it was the American players who took the initiative: on 4 April Glenn Cowan 'accidentally' jumped onto the Chinese team's bus, and after a brief awkward moment, Chinese athlete Zhuang Zedong demonstrated Chinese friendship by offering to the American a silk painting as gift. The following day, Cowan reciprocated with an American T-shirt and, more importantly, expressed his hope of playing in China. After some days of deliberation, Mao gave the go-ahead to the visit of the American ping-pong team, which arrived in China on 10 April. In their week-long stay, the American visitors not only played table tennis with the Chinese players (who were instructed to deliberately lose a few matches), but also toured Beijing and other Chinese cities and got an interview with Premier Zhou. On 14 April Zhou expressed to the American players that 'with your visit, the door to our friendship has been [re]opened'.[11]

China's 'ping-pong diplomacy' immediately paid off. Shortly after Zhou's meeting with the American players, Washington announced a number of new policy measures including the termination of the 22-year-old trade embargo and US currency controls on the PRC. On

27 April, the White House received a handwritten two-page letter from Zhou via the Pakistani ambassador to China, stating that Beijing would welcome a special envoy of the US President, or even the President himself for direct talks. The next month, Nixon replied positively to the Chinese invitation, and in June the two sides agreed to a secret visit by Kissinger in July to discuss Taiwan and other issues of common interest.

Kissinger and Nixon in China

On 9 July, after a secret flight from Islamabad, Kissinger and his small team of aides arrived at Beijing. From 4:35 pm to almost midnight, Kissinger and Zhou discussed Taiwan and other world issues. Well prepared for his trip, Kissinger realized the importance of praising China's long civilization and addressing its unfortunate recent history: 'For the past century you were victims of foreign oppression', but today 'we are both turning a new page in our histories' on 'a basis of equality and mutual respect'. Zhou spelt out the Chinese position directly: in seeking normalization of relations, the United States should recognize the PRC as 'the sole legitimate government of China' and Taiwan 'a Chinese province'. The defence treaty between Washington and Taipei concluded in 1954 was 'illegal', he added.

In response, Kissinger enunciated the US approach towards resolving the Taiwan question by dividing it into two aspects. The first and more immediate aspect concerned 'the military situation in Taiwan and the Taiwan Straits'. Kissinger stated that the United States would remove two-thirds of its armed forces, which were stationed there because of the Vietnam War, from Taiwan after the conclusion of that conflict, and that the remaining one-third, essential to the defence of Taiwan, would be withdrawn as Sino-American relations improved. Concerning the second and long-term aspect – 'the question of political evolution between Taiwan and the PRC' – Kissinger said that the United States was 'not advocating a "two Chinas" solution or a "one China, one Taiwan" solution', and that the 'political evolution' of Taiwan was 'likely to be in the direction' which Zhou had just indicated. Besides, Kissinger asserted that the administration 'would not support' 'the so-called Taiwan Independence Movement'. He reassured Zhou that the United States 'will never collude with other countries against the People's Republic of China, either with our allies or with some of our opponents'.[12]

During Kissinger's three-day stay in Beijing, the Chinese leaders came to realize that the United States would not accept immediate diplomatic recognition of the PRC as a condition for Nixon's visit to

China. Washington would curtail its military and diplomatic links with Taiwan when Sino-American relations improved and regional tensions relaxed during Nixon's second term. Moreover, by linking the gradual US military withdrawal from Taiwan with the end of the Vietnam War, Kissinger wanted Beijing to put pressure on Hanoi so that the United States could withdraw from Vietnam 'with honour'. In short, there remained a great gap between the United States and China as far as Taiwan was concerned. Nevertheless, Kissinger's secret visit allowed each side to understand the other's position and principles. At a personal level, Kissinger and Zhou had developed mutual respect and trust, a rapport which facilitated their subsequent negotiations.[13]

Shortly after Kissinger's departure, a domestic political event occurred, which reinforced Mao's sense of the need for a diplomatic breakthrough with America. On 13 September, Defence Minister Lin Biao and his son and wife were killed in a mysterious plane crash over Mongolia. By that time, Mao had already fallen out with his designated successor due to the perceived growing influence of the armed forces in government. After the plane crash, the 'anti-party' Lin was alleged to have planned to assassinate Mao. The more likely reason, though, was that Lin Liguo, Lin's son, who worried about his father's vulnerable position, had tried but failed to launch a pre-emptive strike against Mao – thus their desperate escape by plane which ended in tragedy. Caught between his paranoid boss and his ambitious son, Lin Biao indeed had no intention to topple the Chairman.[14] Nor did Lin oppose Mao's policy of Sino-American rapprochement, foreign affairs being outside his interest and responsibilities.[15] Whatever the case, Mao approached the Lin Biao Incident with mixed feelings: on the one hand, he was relieved that his perceived political rival had been killed; on the other, the suggestion of an 'anti-party plot' by his chosen successor shattered the myth of Mao's 'eternal correctness'. Mao needed a foreign policy success to rebuild his reputation.[16]

On 20 October Kissinger made his second, and public, visit to Beijing for further talks with Zhou. Among the most important issues to discuss was the drafting of a communiqué to be issued during Nixon's upcoming visit. After 11 hours of discussions over seven drafts, the two sides agreed on a tentative communiqué with the exception of the section on Taiwan.[17] While Kissinger was in Beijing, the UN General Assembly began its annual debate on the question of Chinese representation.

Mao believed that the PRC should take up its lawful seat in the UN. Until 1971, the United States had been using different devices to prevent Communist China from entering the UN – the 'moratorium' procedure to block a UN debate on the question of Chinese representation in the

1950s and the 'important question' resolution that required a two-thirds majority to change the China seat since 1961. But as more Asian-African nations acquired independence in the 1960s, support for China's entry steadily grew. In 1965 the Albanian resolution to give the seat to the PRC and expel the Nationalists produced a tie, and in 1970 the resolution reached a simple majority for the first time.[18]

Nineteen-seventy-one was a critical year for China's entry, for US allies such as Italy, Canada, and Britain had made it clear that they would cast their votes against the resolution of the important question. The Nixon administration's objective thus shifted from opposing China's admission to preventing Taiwan's expulsion. Nevertheless, as the UN debate coincided with Kissinger's public visit to Beijing, the message to all member states could not be clearer. On 25 October, China was voted into the UN by an overwhelming majority of 76 votes to 35 with 17 abstentions. The Nationalist representative walked out of the assembly hall. Mao's China now occupied seats in both the General Assembly and the Security Council.

China's enhanced international status was confirmed by the arrival of President Nixon and his massive entourage on 21 February 1972. Given the historic significance of the presidential visit, Beijing had made extensive preparations to ensure that the American party's public engagements – banquets, sightseeing, photo-opportunities, and so forth – would go smoothly. Nixon, too, attached great importance to the propaganda value of his visit, particularly so in a presidential election year. (A joke circulated within the American press corps that Nixon's primary was in Beijing.)[19] Arriving at Beijing Airport at 11:30 am, Nixon (and his wife) descended the steps from Air Force One alone, walking towards and extending his hand to Premier Zhou. To Nixon (and Mao), the handshake with Zhou was important not only to right the wrong of Secretary of State Dulles' refusing to shake hands with the Premier in 1954 but also to demonstrate to the whole world that China was being treated as an equal by the United States.[20]

On the first evening of their visit, Nixon and Kissinger were invited to meet Mao and Zhou in the Chairman's study. Suffering from heart problems, Mao did not go into details on any specific issues but instead talked about 'philosophical questions' concerning the international situation. But as Chen Jian shrewdly wrote: 'what was most meaningful for the chairman was ... the simple fact that Nixon and Kissinger came to *his* study to listen to *his* teachings.'[21] As the chief architect of China's policy of rapprochement, Mao laid down the principled framework for detailed negotiations between Zhou and Nixon/Kissinger.

During the 1972 summit, both the Chinese and American leaders made compromises over the Taiwan question. '[O]n Taiwan', wrote Yafeng Xia, 'both Kissinger and Zhou seemed firm but flexible.'[22] With Nixon's 'private assurances' on Taiwan, Mao and Zhou were flexible enough to accept the reality of 'one China, one Taiwan for the time being', lest it would create a domestic political backlash for the President. Thus, they accepted that China and America normalized relations in 1972 but Washington would not terminate diplomatic relations with Taiwan until Nixon's second term. Mao agreed that Washington would 'progressively reduce' US forces in Taiwan as regional tension diminished but could not set any 'deadlines'. Beijing no longer insisted on the immediate abrogation of the US–Taiwan Defence Treaty and instead 'let history settle it'. On the other hand, Mao held firm to the principle of national sovereignty and territorial integrity. During the talks, he had given no commitment to a peaceful resolution of the Taiwan problem but only his 'hope' for it. Nor had Mao promised to exert pressure on Hanoi to help the United States withdraw from Vietnam 'with honour'.

On 27 February, the Sino-American Communiqué was issued in Shanghai. The two countries agreed to conduct their relations on the principles of respect for national sovereignty and territorial integrity, non-aggression, non-interference in each other's internal affairs, equality and mutual benefit, and peaceful coexistence. Mao's China was formally admitted to the international community.

Security threat or social-imperialist threat?

Why did Mao fundamentally transform China's relations with the two superpowers in the early 1970s? One view holds that China needed to meet the security threat posed by the Soviets by 'playing the American card'. According to this, Mao was a pragmatic and flexible leader, conducting foreign affairs in terms of balance-of-power and security calculations. The escalating Sino-Soviet border clashes since August 1969 including the possibility of a Soviet nuclear strike were a genuine threat, propelling Beijing to prepare for war. As Yang Kuisong put it, 'it was the perception of an extremely grave threat from the Soviet Union that pushed Mao to decide to break up all existing conceptual restrictions to pursue a Sino-American *rapprochement*'.[23] John Garver also put forward a security argument but with a twist. Arguing that deterring a Soviet attack was not the primary factor behind the Chinese leaders' decision to improve relations with America, it was their perception of major shifts in Asian and global structures of power and their desire to thwart Soviet–American collusion against China that caused them to 'use barbarians to oppose barbarians'.[24]

Chen Jian, on the other hand, has challenged the strategic/geopolitical interpretation by explaining the Sino-American rapprochement within the context of Mao's fading 'continuous revolution'. To Mao, the Soviet Union was not merely a conventional military threat to China's physical security. More importantly, as a 'social-imperialist country', the Soviet Union posed an ideological threat even greater than the American imperialists. What is more, Mao decided to normalize relations with Washington at a time when his project of 'continuous revolution' was fading. Especially after the Lin Biao Incident, which had damaged the myth of his 'eternal correctness', Mao needed a major diplomatic breakthrough in China's foreign relations to salvage his declining reputation and authority. Thus, as Chen wrote, 'the Sino-American rapprochement was less a case in which ideological beliefs yielded to the security interests than one in which ideology ... experienced subtle structural changes as the result of the fading status of Mao's continuous revolution'.[25]

This book argues that ideology and security should be seen not in dichotomous terms but as mutually reinforcing factors behind Chinese foreign policy. In 1972 Mao redefined China's identity as a 'friend' of America for the sake of national security and his fading ideological project.

Notes

1 Roderick MacFarquhar and Michael Schoenhals, *Mao's Last Revolution* (Cambridge, Mass.: Harvard University Press, 2006), 285–301.
2 Unless otherwise stated, this section draws on Yang Kuisong, 'The Sino-Soviet Border Clash of 1969: From Zhenbao Island to Sino-American Rapprochement', *CWH* 1: 1 (August 2000): 21–52.
3 Lyle J. Goldstein, 'Return to Zhenbao Island: Who Started Shooting and Why it Matters', *CQ* 168 (December 2001): 991–4.
4 MacFarquhar and Schoenhals, op. cit., 317–19.
5 On Kissinger's diplomatic thinking and practice, see Jussi M Hanhimäki, *The Flawed Architect: Henry Kissinger and American Foreign Policy* (Oxford: Oxford University Press, 2004).
6 On the Chinese perspective, see Chen Jian, *Mao's China and the Cold War* (Chapel Hill: The University of North Carolina Press, 2001), 238–76; Gong Li, 'Chinese Decision Making and the Thawing of U.S.–China Relations', in Ross and Jiang (eds), *Re-examining the Cold War*, 321–60; Yafeng Xia, *Negotiating with the Enemy: US–China Talks during the Cold War, 1949–1972* (Bloomington: Indiana University Press, 2006), Chapters 6–8.
7 Report by the Four Marshals, 17 September 1969, in *CWIHPB* 11 (Winter 1998), 170.

8 Chen, op. cit., 249.
9 Ibid., 254–7.
10 Quoted in Xia, op. cit., 151.
11 Xu Guoqi, *Olympic Dreams: China and Sports, 1895–2008* (Cambridge, Mass: Harvard University Press, 2008), 117–19, 126–40. Quotation on 138.
12 *FRUS, 1969–1976*, vol. xvii: *China, 1969–1972* (Washington, D.C.: Government Printing Office, 2006), 365–72.
13 Xia, op. cit., 165–74.
14 MacFarquhar and Schoenhals, op. cit., 324–36.
15 See Xia Yafeng, 'China's Elite Politics and Sino-American Rapprochement, January 1969–February 1972', *JCWS* 8: 4 (Autumn 2006): 3–28.
16 Chen, op. cit., 270.
17 *FRUS, 1969–1976*, vol. xvii, 559–70.
18 See Rosemary Foot, *The Practice of Power: US Relations with China since 1949* (Oxford: Clarendon Press, 1995), 24–46.
19 For the public activities of Nixon's party in China, see Margaret Macmillan, *Seize the Hour: When Nixon Met Mao* (London: John Murray, 2006), 145–57, 266–79.
20 Ibid., 33.
21 Chen, op. cit., 273.
22 Xia, op. cit., 188.
23 Yang, op. cit., 46.
24 John W. Garver, *China's Decision for Rapprochement with the United States, 1968–1971* (Boulder: Westview Press, 1982).
25 Chen, op. cit., 242.

7 Mao's last diplomatic struggle and anti-hegemony, 1972–8

Between 1972 and 1978, China's relations with the world entered a period of transitional change. While China and the United States no longer saw each other as Cold War adversaries, there were twists and turns in their relationship, thanks to divergent views on the Soviet threat and the Taiwan question. From 1974 on, Mao re-emphasized China's Third World identity, a key component of which was anti-hegemony. Domestically, the two prominent first-generation leaders, Zhou Enlai and Mao, died in the course of 1976. Succession politics complicated the making of foreign policy.

Third wave of diplomatic recognition

The first half of the 1970s saw the third wave of diplomatic recognition. From 50 on the eve of the Cultural Revolution, the number of countries having diplomatic relations with China doubled to almost 100 by the end of 1974. In 1972 alone, 18 countries established diplomatic relations with the PRC. Unlike the first and second waves of recognition, which included primarily Communist countries and newly independent Afro-Asian nations respectively, the third wave was characterized by diplomatic breakthrough with developed countries in Western Europe and North America, for example Italy, West Germany, Canada, and Britain.

China also established diplomatic relations with Japan in 1972. Prior to the Sino-American rapprochement, China's political relations with Japan had been constrained by the 1952 Peace Treaty between Japan and Taiwan and the US–Japan alliance, notwithstanding the development of Sino-Japanese economic relations. Beijing resented Prime Minister Sato Eisaku's fervent support for Taiwan, and worried about the revival of Japanese militarism in the light of America's disengagement from Vietnam. It insisted on three principles for Sino-Japanese reconciliation: that Tokyo should recognize the PRC as the sole legitimate government of

China and Taiwan as China's province, and that the Japan–Taiwan Treaty was unlawful and should be abolished.[1] During the high-level talks in China, Kissinger and Nixon had reassured the Chinese leaders that the United States opposed the revival of Japanese militarism, especially in Taiwan, while justifying the continued American military presence in Japan as a restraining force on Tokyo. With the replacement of Sato by Tanaka Kakuei in July, the Chinese government became more flexible over the terms of establishing diplomatic relations with Japan. It agreed not to include a direct reference to the Japan–Taiwan Peace Treaty in the Sino-Japanese communiqué (lest it should create a political backlash in Japan), and instead put its 'trust' in the new Japanese Prime Minister. On 29 September, Beijing and Tokyo signed a joint communiqué on the establishment of diplomatic relations. The same day, the Japanese Foreign Minister announced that, as a 'result' of Sino-Japanese normalization, the Japan–Taiwan Peace Treaty 'has lost its *raison d'être* and can be considered terminated'.[2]

After diplomatic normalization, China's foreign economic relations with the major capitalist countries flourished. Between 1972 and 1973, China's exports to Japan doubled in value, from US$411.8 million to US$841.1 million, while its imports increased from US$627.4 million to US$1,107.5 million. Japan became China's leading trading partner and remained so for the whole decade. Sino-American bilateral trade also grew, although lagging behind Japan, Britain, and European countries such as West Germany.[3] But it was geopolitics not economics that played a decisive role in shaping Sino-American relations during the 1970s.

China in the strategic triangle

The year after Nixon's visit could be deemed the 'honeymoon' period of the new Sino-American relationship. No sooner had he left China than Nixon ordered the withdrawal of US nuclear-capable bomber units from Taiwan. Kissinger made frequent visits to Beijing to exchange views with the Chinese leaders and to promote Sino-American cooperation. Non-governmental exchanges in culture, science, and other fields increased, as did trade between the two countries. As Kissinger described the new relationship to Nixon following his trip to Beijing in June: 'the Chinese have moved ... from an adversary posture to one which can only be described as tacit ally.'[4]

The first clear manifestation of Sino-American cooperation was the end of the Vietnam War. On 27 January 1973, the Paris Peace Agreement on Vietnam was signed. It provided for a ceasefire and the release of

American POWs, thereby facilitating the US military withdrawal from South Vietnam. During their talks in 1971 and 1972, Kissinger and Nixon had repeatedly tried to get Chinese help in ending the Vietnam War by linking it to the withdrawal of US forces from Taiwan. Kissinger argued that there should be a transitional period between the US military withdrawal from Indochina and the 'political evolution' in South Vietnam – or the so-called 'decent interval' solution. If the Vietnamese people wanted to remove Thieu after an interval of several years, Kissinger hinted, the United States would not intervene in the political development of Vietnam. Mao and Zhou, however, objected to any Chinese meddling in Vietnamese affairs, insisting instead that Washington remove the South Vietnamese leader, Nguyen Van Thieu, from power as a precondition for peace in Indochina.[5]

By late 1972, however, Beijing's attitude had softened: it dropped its demand for the removal of Thieu as a precondition for peace. In December that year and early January 1973, the Chinese urged the North Vietnamese to undertake serious negotiation with the Americans in Paris – thus the signing of the Paris Agreement. Did China betray North Vietnam as a result of the Sino-American rapprochement, as Hanoi later alleged? Indeed, as the latest archival evidence shows, not only had Mao and Zhou refused to yield to the Americans concerning Vietnam during their summit talks, but they briefed the North Vietnamese leaders on the latest development of Sino-American rapprochement and continued to provide massive economic and military aid to Hanoi. With Chinese (and Soviet) aid, in March Hanoi launched a 'spring offensive' against South Vietnam, which, however, triggered massive US air bombing and naval blockade of the North in the following months. In view of the escalating war, the Chinese leaders concluded that a diplomatic solution that would expedite the US military withdrawal, even if it meant the preservation of Thieu in Saigon, served the best interests of North Vietnam and China. After the Americans left South Vietnam, they estimated, Thieu would be too weak to stay in power for long.[6]

The first part of 1973 saw not only the (temporary) restoration of peace in Vietnam, but also the institutionalization of the Sino-American dialogues. A liaison office, which performed the functions of an official embassy and enjoyed diplomatic privileges, was set up in each capital. The US Liaison Office in Beijing and the Chinese Liaison Office in Washington began operation on 1 May.

In the course of 1973 and 1974, China's views on the Soviet threat increasingly diverged from America's. After the 1969 border clashes, China remained concerned about the Soviet military presence on the border, which increased from 21 to 45 divisions by 1973. During Kissinger's visit on 17 February, Mao proposed that the two countries should 'draw a horizontal line through the United States, Japan, China, Pakistan, Iran, Turkey and Europe'. Calling it a 'horizontal line' (*yitiaoxian*) strategy, Mao aimed to create an international united front against the Soviet Union. The inclusion of Japan was particularly striking, for Mao's attitude had been fundamentally transformed from his previous fear of revived Japanese militarism to his new view of Japan as an 'incipient ally' to counter the Soviet and Indian designs for the region.[7]

The United States, however, preferred a different approach towards meeting the Soviet threat. Obsessed with the 'strategic triangle' and linkage politics, Kissinger relied on US–Soviet détente as a means of restraining Moscow, while simultaneously pursuing Sino-American normalization to exert additional pressure on the Kremlin. Shortly after his China trip, in June 1972, Nixon landed in Moscow to sign with Leonid Brezhnev the Strategic Arms Limitation Talks (SALT) I Agreement. A year later, another Nixon–Brezhnev summit resulted in the signing of the Basic Principles of Negotiations on Strategic Arms Limitation and the Agreement on the Prevention of Nuclear War. On the other hand, Kissinger tried to maintain the momentum of Sino-American rapprochement. During his China visits, Kissinger increasingly played the 'Soviet card' by exaggerating the Soviet threat to China's security and offering strategic intelligence and later US advanced technology to China. But Mao and Zhou were suspicious of Washington's real intentions, namely the use of China as leverage against the Soviet Union. Rather than supporting Beijing's 'horizontal line' strategy against Moscow, they objected, the United States pursued a policy of appeasing the Soviets in the West, which would free them from expansion in the East.[8]

Domestic politics in China, moreover, cast a shadow over Sino-American relations. After the shock of the Lin Biao Incident, the pragmatists had regained the upper hand over the radicals in politics. With Mao's full support, Zhou was in charge of the day-to-day work of the Party and government. But in his efforts to rehabilitate veteran comrades and to correct the 'mistakes' of the Cultural Revolution, Zhou incurred the wrath of the radicals and even Mao himself. In early March 1973, Zhou, suffering from stomach cancer, recommended to Mao that Deng Xiaoping, who had been purged at the onset of the Cultural Revolution, should resume his Party and government duties. Mao agreed, and the Tenth Party Congress in August rehabilitated Deng. In early 1974, with Mao's approval, Jiang Qing and Wang Hongwen launched the 'Criticize Lin Biao, Criticize Confucius' Campaign, whose real target was Zhou. Aware of the severe illness of Zhou and increasingly dissatisfied with his handling of Sino-American relations, Mao turned to Deng to run the country. By early 1975, Deng's political comeback was complete: he was Vice-Premier, Vice-Chairman of the Politburo Standing Committee, and the Chief of Staff, assuming full responsibility for the daily management of China's foreign policy.[9]

Nevertheless, during 1974 and 1975, decision-making at the top remained complicated, and Sino-American relations suffered as a result. It was due to Mao's ill health and the power struggle among his possible successors. What added to the uncertainty of succession politics was the fact that Mao himself often 'vacillated between the pragmatists and the ultra-leftists'. On the one hand, he was eager to restore order and to check the ultra-leftist influence in China; on the other, he realized that too close an alignment with the pragmatic force would negate the theoretical basis of his Great Proletarian Cultural Revolution.[10] In consequence, the pragmatists in charge of foreign affairs could not afford to appear too soft in dealing with the Americans, particularly concerning Taiwan, lest they should become targets of criticism by the radicals and even Mao. That was the case during Kissinger's visit in late November 1974. In a meeting on 26 November, a tough and adamant Deng 'fired cannon' at Kissinger by stressing Mao's views that 'the solving of the Taiwan question is an internal affair of China, and should be left to the Chinese to solve'.[11] Unlike Zhou, Deng lacked rapport with Kissinger. But the upcoming meeting of the National People's Congress in early 1975, which would determine the new leadership, was probably another factor behind Deng's 'cannon-firing' at Kissinger.

It was US domestic politics that greatly hindered the progress of Sino-American normalization. In April 1974, the Watergate scandal began to unfold and Nixon's hands were tied. It culminated in Nixon's resignation on 9 August and his replacement by the then Vice-President Gerald Ford. Once in power, Ford was confronted with a host of difficult tasks – an emerging economic recession, his pardon of Nixon which aroused public criticism, and above all his bid for the 1976 presidential election. Besides, he faced challenges from the Republican conservatives and particularly the anti-communist Ronald Reagan, who equally had an eye on the Republican presidential nomination. Under these circumstances, Ford could not but have second thoughts on the politically sensitive Taiwan question.

In April 1975 the South Vietnamese government was overthrown by the Vietnamese Communists. With the collapse of Saigon, the United

States could not afford to be seen as selling yet another ally down the river. Ford and Kissinger realized that a complete rupture of diplomatic relations with Taipei would be too heavy a political price to pay for the establishment of Sino-American diplomatic relations. Ford decided to delay normalization until after the 1976 presidential election. He also intended to reaffirm US commitment to Taiwan, namely by setting up a liaison office on the island after withdrawing diplomatic recognition and seeking Beijing's guarantees for a peaceful resolution of the Taiwan question. To convey these new considerations to Mao, Ford sent Kissinger to Beijing in October and made his own China journey in December. The Chinese leaders, however, expressed vehement objections to Ford's significant retrogression from Nixon's pledges. They insisted on three conditions for Sino-American diplomatic normalization: that the United States should sever diplomatic relations with Taiwan, withdraw the remaining US troops from the island, and abrogate the US–Taiwan Defence Treaty. Notwithstanding Ford's agreement to the sale of jet engines and high-speed computers to pacify Beijing, it is clear that Sino-American negotiation over diplomatic relations had reached an impasse.[12]

Mao's three worlds theory

In view of the stagnant Sino-American relationship, Mao reassessed China's diplomatic orientation and global strategy. In 1974, Mao formally put forward the Theory of Three Worlds. In a talk with the President of Zambia on 22 February, Mao claimed that 'three worlds' existed. The 'First World' included the United States and the Soviet Union, both of which possessed 'a lot of atomic bombs' and were 'richer'. The 'Second World' consisted of Japan, Europe, Australia and Canada, all of which did 'not possess so many atomic bombs' and were 'not so rich' as the 'First World'. All Asian countries with the exception of Japan and all of Africa and Latin America, Mao asserted, belonged to the 'Third World', which was 'very populous'.[13] Later in April, Mao asked Deng to head the Chinese delegation to a special session of the UN General Assembly to unveil the Theory of Three Worlds to a global audience. After differentiating the 'three worlds', Deng said: 'The two superpowers are the largest international exploiters and oppressors – the origins of new world war ... Collusion and compromise [between them] are partial, temporary and relative. Contention is total, long-term and absolute.' 'It is not the two superpowers who are really powerful,' Deng continued, 'rather it is those people from the third world countries who unite and dare to fight and win.'[14]

Although the existence of 'contradictions' between the two super-powers and the rest of the world was not an entirely new concept, Mao's formulation of the Three Worlds Theory in the critical year of 1974 was of great strategic significance. The Three Worlds Theory was a fundamental departure from the 'horizontal line strategy, proposed by Mao in early 1973, in that it called for the formation of an international anti-hegemony united front against both the Soviet Union and the United States. By early 1974, the 'honeymoon' of Sino-American relations was over. Strategically, Mao was suspicious of Washington's real motive behind rapprochement, which was to use China primarily as leverage against the Soviet Union in the 'strategic triangle'. Ideologically and psychologically, the Chairman never felt comfortable about reconciliation with the American imperialists: he was struggling between détente with Washington and support for world revolution.[15] Thus, China needed to confront both superpowers, which were competing for global hegemony, in a broad united front with all developed and developing countries.

The Three Worlds Theory, moreover, provided the ideological justification for reasserting China's identity as a developing nation and its identification with the 'revolutionary' cause of the world's oppressed peoples. But the emphasis was no longer on assistance to national liberation movements on the basis of 'class struggles' (although Beijing did not end its moral and material aid to all foreign communist parties and insurgencies). Rather, in the 1970s, 'revolution' for China meant 'overturning the old international order founded on dual superpower hegemony, and creating a new, qualitatively different international order based on absolute equality of all nations, and strict respect for the Five Principles of Peaceful Coexistence'. To Mao, countries, not classes, were the main agent of change in the emerging multipolar international system. Diplomacy, not armed struggle, was China's main instrument to promote multipolarity.[16]

Under the guidance of Mao's Three Worlds Theory, the PRC sought to expand its diplomatic space in the Third World. In 1974 China established diplomatic relations with Malaysia, and the next year, with Thailand and the Philippines. On the other hand, Beijing lent support to Third World nations in their struggles to win or maintain national independence. It opposed South African racism including the 'reactionary' regime of Rhodesia and the apartheid policy of South Africa. It condemned Israel's regional hegemonism against the Palestinians and the Arab countries.

Perhaps the most 'revolutionary' aspect of China's Third World diplomacy in the 1970s was its involvement in the creation of a New

International Economic Order. Indeed, the initiative came not from China but from a group of Third World developing countries, or the Group of 77 (later expanded to over 100), within the UN Conference on Trade and Development, which aimed at a redistribution of global wealth. At the 1974 UN special session in which he unveiled the Three Worlds Theory, Deng not only called for world-wide opposition to the superpowers' bid for political hegemony but also talked at great length about the importance of restructuring the existing inequitable international economic order on the principles of equality and mutual benefit. As Deng claimed, 'political independence and economic independence are inseparable ... In both political and economic relations, countries should base themselves on the well-known Five Principles of Peaceful Coexistence.' Specifically, Deng argued that the developing countries should have 'permanent sovereignty' over their own natural resources; economic aid to the developing countries should not be accompanied by any conditions; and loans should be interest-free or low-interest.[17]

Nevertheless, one should not exaggerate China's role in the creation of a New International Economic Order. Despite being invited, China declined to join the Group of 77. As far as the UN as a whole was concerned, China played largely 'a cautious, modest, and self-effacing role' in those organs and activities of the UN in which it participated. The Chinese delegation kept a rather low profile, and seldom initiated proposals or exercised vetoes. The PRC's participation in the UN, though, was of 'symbolic and political significance', enhancing the image, prestige, and legitimacy of the organization, and vice versa.[18]

Post-Mao succession politics and Sino-American normalization

Mao's diplomatic struggle against the Soviet and American hegemonies ended prematurely. On 8 January 1976, Zhou died. In April students, workers, and common Beijingers gathered at Tiananmen Square to commemorate their beloved premier. The gathering soon turned into mass protest and eventually brutal suppression by the authorities. Deng, accused of masterminding the 'counter-revolutionary riots', was purged a second time by the dying Mao. On 9 September, Mao died at the age of 82. Hua Guofeng succeeded him as Party Chairman, and quickly arrested the Gang of Four headed by Jiang Qing. In July–August 1977, Deng was rehabilitated, taking over the portfolios of defence and foreign affairs. Behind the scenes, the struggle for supreme power between Hua, a 'whateverist' who stubbornly followed whatever policy Mao had adopted, and Deng, a pragmatist who advocated economic reform and an open-door policy, was unfolding. In the United

States, Ford failed in his presidential election bid in November 1976, and Jimmy Carter was elected president. Preoccupied with the political change in 1976, neither the Chinese nor the American leaders devoted adequate attention to the question of diplomatic normalization.

It was the changing perceptions of the Soviet threat on the part of both Beijing and Washington from late 1977 onwards that provided renewed impetus for Sino-American normalization. Despite Brezhnev's message of condolence and wishes for improved relations following Mao's death, the Soviet Union maintained heavy military presence along the Sino-Soviet and Sino-Mongolian borders. Moreover, it expanded the Pacific Fleet, and conducted frequent military exercises close to China. In addition to these, the Soviet Union increased its military ties with Vietnam, whose relations with China were increasingly strained over Beijing's withdrawal of economic aid and Hanoi's mistreatment of its ethnic Chinese residents. With Moscow's endorsement, Vietnam invaded Cambodia in late 1978, partly to remove the murderous Pol Pot regime backed by Beijing. To the post-Mao leadership, Vietnam was a threat to China's national security, and the United States was regarded as a counterweight to Hanoi's regional hegemony supported by Moscow.[19]

The Carter administration, for its part, was alarmed by Soviet adventurism in the Horn of Africa and Cambodia/Vietnam, as well as Moscow's uncompromising stance at strategic arms limitation talks. Carter and his national security advisor, Zbigniew Brzezinski, decided to reinvigorate the US–China strategic partnership against the Soviet Union. In July 1978, secret talks on the establishment of diplomatic relations started. The differences between America and China boiled down to three issues: the maintenance of some form of US representation in Taiwan after withdrawing diplomatic recognition; the termination of the US–Taiwan Defence Treaty; and the question of US arms sales to Taiwan.[20]

Eventually, the United States and China each made compromises out of consideration of each other's internal political situation.[21] Carter and Brzezinski were not unaware of Deng's delicate position *vis-à-vis* Hua in the succession struggle. A foreign policy success, they calculated, would boost the reform-oriented Deng and hopefully open the potential Chinese market to US goods and investment after Deng became the supreme leader. Likewise, Deng realized that China needed US technology and capital for its economic modernization, but US domestic politics concerning Taiwan was a hindrance. Thus, Deng acquiesced to the termination of the US–Taiwan Defence Treaty a year after (rather than at the same time as) Sino-American normalization, and deferred the resolution of the question of US arms sales to Taiwan (while reserving the right to raise it later). Carter, in turn, agreed to stop US arms sales to Taiwan for one year (when the Defence Treaty remained in effect), and to invite Deng or a top Chinese leader for a state visit to the United States.[22]

On 15 December, without prior notice to Congress, the Carter administration announced that the United States would recognize the PRC as the 'sole legal government of China', effective from 1 January 1979, and would terminate the US–Taiwan Defence Treaty in a year's time, while maintaining 'commercial, cultural and other relations' with Taiwan 'without official government representation and without diplomatic relations'. On 1 January 1979, Washington and Beijing issued a joint communiqué on establishing diplomatic relations, which stated that neither country should seek 'hegemony' in the Asia-Pacific or in the wider world. Together with the 1972 Shanghai Communiqué, the 1979 communiqué provided a legal framework of major principles for governing Sino-American relations for years to come.[23]

Strategic triangle or domestic politics?

Why did Sino-American normalization experience twists and turns between 1972 and 1978? One line of explanation centres on the impact of the 'strategic triangle' on China's security and diplomacy. As Robert Ross puts it, 'China's relative weakness vis-à-vis both the superpowers, the corresponding magnitude of the Soviet threat, and the significance of security cooperation with the United States were the dominant strategic factors shaping Beijing's participation in US–Soviet–PRC interactions.'[24] As the weakest power of the three, China was constrained by the logic and dynamics of the 'strategic triangle'. In the two years or so after Nixon's visit, China needed to cooperate with the United States to counter the Soviet threat, but it was not in a position to coerce Washington into supporting Mao's confrontational 'horizontal line' strategy. By 1974, suspicious of Washington's real motives, China lost enthusiasm for Sino-American strategic cooperation and instead sought to construct an international anti-hegemony united front with developed and developing countries in accordance with Mao's Three Worlds Theory. Only when China's international security environment deteriorated in 1977–8, as a result of Soviet and Vietnamese hegemonic expansion, did Beijing revive interest in strategic cooperation with Washington (which was equally alarmed by Moscow's adventurism) and expedite the negotiations over Sino-American normalization.

Another explanation focuses on the impact of domestic politics, especially during 1974–6. From 1974 on, Zhou's fatal illness and Mao's deteriorating heath triggered the behind-the-scenes succession power struggle. Deng was rehabilitated by Mao to manage the day-to-day work of the Party and government as well as foreign policy. But aware of the radicals' criticism, Deng could not afford to appear 'soft' in negotiating with the Americans over the Taiwan question – thus, the lack of progress on Sino-American normalization during 1974–5. By 1977–8, domestic politics once again made their impact felt on Deng's approach to Sino-American negotiations – but with a reverse twist. As Li Jie argues, for the pragmatic Deng, '[n]ormalization of Sino-US relations was now necessary not only for maintaining national security in the Cold War but also for implementing the strategy of reform and opening up.'[25] Taking into account the domestic political difficulties faced by the Carter administration, Deng was willing to compromise over the terms of Sino-American normalization, such as deferring the sensitive question of US arms sales to Taiwan. Enrico Fardella similarly stresses the role of domestic politics: 'The "domestic" effects of the normalization were key issues in how negotiations were closed ... Chinese domestic policy became an integral part of the administration's China policy and, at the same time, American domestic policy became a crucial factor within Deng's strategy.'[26]

Notes

1 Yoshihide Soeya, *Japan's Economic Diplomacy with China, 1945–1978* (Oxford: Clarendon Press, 1998), 109–13.
2 Han Nianlong *et al.*, *Diplomacy of Contemporary China* (Hong Kong: New Horizon Press, 1990), 362.
3 Lawrence C. Reardon, *The Reluctant Dragon: Crisis Cycles in Chinese Foreign Economic Policy* (Hong Kong: Hong Kong University Press, 2002), 149–51.
4 Quoted in Evelyn Goh, *Constructing the U.S. Rapprochement with China, 1961–1974: From 'Red Menace' to 'Tacit Ally'* (New York: Cambridge University Press, 2005), 223.
5 See Chris Connolly, 'The American Factor: Sino-American Rapprochement and Chinese Attitudes to the Vietnam War, 1968–72', *CWH* 5: 4 (November 2005): 501–27.
6 Lorenz M. Luthi, 'Beyond Betrayal: Beijing, Moscow, and the Paris Negotiations, 1971–73', *JCWS* 11: 1 (Winter 2009): 57–107.
7 Gong Li, 'The Difficult Path to Diplomatic Relations: China's U.S. Policy, 1972–78', in William C. Kirby, Robert S. Ross, Gong Li (eds), *Normalization of U.S.–China Relations: An International History* (Cambridge, Mass.: Harvard University Press, 2006), 122.
8 Goh, op. cit., 227–43.

9 See Li Jie, 'China's Domestic Politics and the Normalization of Sino-U.S. Relations, 1969–79', in Kirby and others (eds), op. cit., 63–77.

10 Ibid., 78.

11 William Burr (ed.), *The Kissinger Transcripts: The Top Secret Talks with Beijing and Moscow* (New York: The New Press, 1998), 298.

12 Gong, op. cit., 127–33.

13 *Mao Zedong on Diplomacy*, 454.

14 Quoted in Kuisong Yang and Yafeng Xia, 'Vacillating between Revolution and Détente: Mao's Changing Psyche and Policy toward the United States, 1969–76', *DH* 34: 2 (April 2010): 418.

15 On this theme, see ibid., 395–423.

16 John Garver, *Foreign Relations of the People's Republic of China* (Englewood Cliffs, N.J.: Prentice Hall, 1993), 166–7.

17 Han *et al.*, op. cit., 322–5.

18 Samuel S. Kim, *China, the United Nations, and World Order* (Princeton: Princeton University Press, 1979), 177, 199.

19 Wang Zhongchun, 'The Soviet Factor in Sino-American Normalization, 1969–79', in Kirby and others (eds), op. cit., 165–6.

20 Gong, op. cit., 137–44.

21 On this argument, see Enrico Fardella, 'The Sino-American Normalization: A Reassessment', *DH* 33: 4 (September 2009): 545–78.

22 Robert Ross, *Negotiating Cooperation: The United States and China, 1969–1989* (Stanford: Stanford University Press, 1995), 134–41.

23 See Harry Harding, *A Fragile Relationship: The United States and China since 1972* (Washington, D.C.: The Brookings Institution, 1992), 379–81.

24 Robert S. Ross, 'Conclusion: Tripolarity and Policy Making', in Robert S. Ross (ed.), *China, the United States, and the Soviet Union: Tripolarity and Policy Making in the Cold War* (Armonk: M. E. Sharpe, 1993), 183.

25 Li, op. cit., 82.

26 Fardella, op. cit., 546.

8 Post-Mao economic reform and independent foreign policy, 1979–89

In late 1978 Deng Xiaoping emerged as the paramount leader of the CCP, beginning the fundamental transformation of China's economy and society as well as foreign policy. Following the establishment of diplomatic relations in 1979, Deng consolidated Sino-American cooperation at all levels. In 1982, concerned about the international and domestic implications of a complete tilt towards America, Deng proclaimed an 'independent foreign policy', whereby China would seek an even-handed approach towards the two superpowers. During the 1980s, Deng was redefining China's national identity in the age of unprecedented economic reform and relaxed international tension.

Economic reforms

Deng became the nucleus of the second generation of CCP leadership from late 1978 onwards. Prior to that, his main political rival was Hua Guofeng, who succeeded Zhou Enlai as Premier and Mao Zedong as Party Chairman. At the Eleventh Party Congress in August 1977, Deng was elected Vice-Chairman of the CCP, while also managing government and military affairs in his capacities as Vice-Premier and Chairman of the Central Military Commission (both Party and state). At the third plenum of the Eleventh Party Congress on 18–22 December 1978, Deng finally prevailed over Hua, and his policy of economic reform and opening-up was adopted. Thereafter, Deng strove to build a reform-oriented 'nuclear core' centred on him. In late December, Hu Yaobang was appointed to the new post of Secretary General of the CCP Central Committee. In February 1980 Hu and Zhao Ziyang were elected to the Politburo Standing Committee, and three of the 'whateverists' were stripped of their memberships. Politically isolated, Hua was gradually forced to give up his two main posts. In September,

Zhao took over the premiership; in June 1981, Hu became the Party Chairman (renamed General Secretary in 1982).

It is worth noting that Deng chose not to take up formal titles himself. Rather, he stepped down as Vice-Premier in 1980; during the Thirteenth Party Congress in 1987, he announced 'voluntary retirement' from all Party posts, retaining only the chairmanship of the Central Military Commission. Nevertheless, Deng remained the ultimate decision-maker. Indeed, the first plenum of the Thirteenth Party Congress adopted a secret resolution stipulating that Deng had to be consulted on all crucial decisions. Although lacking the absolute authority that Mao once commanded, Deng indeed belonged to the first generation of CCP revolutionary leaders: in foreign affairs, he had played a major role in the Sino-Soviet polemics in the late 1950s and early 1960s and in the Sino-American normalization negotiations in the early 1970s. With his rich experience and senior status, Deng was the chief architect of China's economic and foreign policy during the 1980s.[1]

Deng's project of economic reform was devised and carried out in a gradual, piecemeal manner. The origins of the reform could be traced back to Zhou's idea of the 'Four Modernizations' – agriculture, industry, science and technology, and national defence – outlined in early 1975. In February 1978, Party Chairman Hua Guofeng unveiled an ambitious ten-year modernization programme. Nevertheless, it was not until Deng's rise to a paramount position in December that the key decisions on accelerating China's economic development and opening the country to the outside world were formally adopted.[2] As Deng proclaimed: 'Reform is China's second revolution.'[3] Despite the lack of an overall blueprint at the time, Deng called for the nation to 'emancipate the mind' and to 'seek truth from facts'. Deng's economic pragmatism was best captured by his famous 'cat theory': whether 'black cat or white cat', 'as long as it catches mice, it is a good cat'.

Domestically, reform began in the rural sector and in poorer regions such as Anhui. The Maoist model of central planning was replaced by economic decentralization and the market mechanism. Through the introduction of the household responsibility system and the development of rural enterprises, Deng aimed to increase agricultural productivity and rural incomes, which could help finance the development of the urban economy.

As far as opening China to the world economy was concerned, Deng's reform centred on the establishment of Special Economic Zones (SEZs), the import of advanced technology, and encouragement of foreign direct investment and foreign trade. In 1979 SEZs were set up at Shenzhen, Zhuhai, Xiamen, and Shantou, all of which were close to the Overseas Chinese communities of Hong Kong, Macao, and Taiwan, not only geographically but also in familial and cultural terms. Deng conceived the SEZs as a relatively isolated economic laboratory in which the Chinese experimented with Western capitalist ideas and practice. Through special tax and tariff incentives, provision of infrastructure, and the availability of a cheap labour force, the SEZs were designed to attract foreign advanced technology and direct investment, increase China's exports, and earn foreign exchange. In 1984, 14 coastal cities and the Hainan Island were also opened to foreign economic operations.

With the intensification of the reform, the pattern of China's foreign trade underwent significant change. Between 1979 and 1989, China's total trade in absolute terms increased by almost ten times, from 45.5 to 415.6 billion yuan, and as a percentage of GNP more than doubled, from 11.4 to 26.3 per cent. Trade with Hong Kong, Japan, the United States, and Western Europe all grew enormously. In the case of Hong Kong, enterprising Chinese businessmen took full advantage of the policy of SEZs by shifting their light manufacturing operations to South China, particularly Guangdong Province. By 1989, Hong Kong topped China's major trading partner, followed by Japan and the United States.[4] China exported mainly agricultural products, textiles, and light industrial goods such as bicycles and sewing machines, and imported sophisticated machinery, advanced technology, and manufactured goods.

Post-normalization Sino-American relations

In January 1979, the Chinese and US governments issued a joint communiqué on establishing diplomatic relations. Angered by the lack of prior consultation on the terms of normalization, on 10 April the US Congress passed unanimously the Taiwan Relations Act, stipulating that the United States would 'consider any effort to determine the future of Taiwan by other than peaceful means ... a threat to peace and security of the Western Pacific area and of grave concern to the United States' and would 'provide Taiwan with arms of a defensive character'.[5] President Carter quickly reassured Deng that he had substantial discretion in interpreting and implementing the law in ways that would be fully consistent with the previous US–China understandings.[6] Although antagonized by the passage of the Taiwan Relations Act, Deng felt that the US Congress could not stand in the way of Sino-American strategic cooperation, which had been demonstrated in his successful state visit to the United States and Carter's acquiescence in China's war against Vietnam.

Between 28 January and 5 February 1979, Deng made a high-profile visit to America. From Washington to Atlanta to Houston (where he caught the world's imagination by waving a ten-gallon hat at a Texas rodeo), Deng made good use of every public engagement and photo opportunity to cement Sino-American friendship and his domestic political authority. But both Deng and Carter also had important business to discuss in private. As for the President, the fall of the pro-Western Shah in Iran as a result of the Islamic revolution had cost Washington two vital intelligence collection stations for monitoring Soviet nuclear and missile tests, and necessitated replacement sites. During his talks with Brzezinski, Deng agreed to the setting-up of new signals-intelligence stations in western China, which would be installed and managed by US intelligence officers (with Chinese help) and whose collected intelligence would be shared.[7]

Deng, for his part, needed American moral support for China's 'self-defensive counter-attack' against Vietnam. By early 1979, Sino-Vietnamese relations had reached an all-time low as a result of the Vietnamese invasion of Cambodia, Hanoi's expulsion of ethnic Chinese residents, and the growing border clashes. Having provided massive military and economic assistance to Hanoi in the previous two decades, Beijing felt 'betrayed' and wanted to 'teach Vietnam a lesson'. In a close session with Deng (and an interpreter), Carter 'handed Deng a note that simply urged restraint in what even Brzezinski acknowledged would be overt military aggression'.[8] Having secured Carter's 'green light', upon his return from the United States, Deng made the final decision on a limited war against Vietnam. Starting on 17 February and lasting for 17 days, more than a quarter-million PLA troops attacked the Vietnamese forces, occupying land but suffering heavy casualties themselves. On 5 March, Beijing announced the withdrawal of the Chinese troops. To Deng, the chief geopolitical objective of 'teaching Vietnam a lesson' had been achieved.[9]

The strengthening of Sino-American strategic cooperation went far beyond Carter's acquiescence in China's Vietnam operations. With Brzezinski's encouragement, the administration relaxed its restrictions on the export of advanced technology to China on a case-by-case basis, although the ban on US arms sales remained in force. Following the Soviet invasion of Afghanistan in December, Sino-American military ties were expanded. An agreement on the exchange of visits by high-level defence officials was reached. An active programme of intelligence sharing, especially concerning Soviet deployments in the Far East, was put in place.[10]

Sino-American economic and cultural relations, too, flourished. In the summer of 1979, the Carter administration decided to extend the most-favoured-nation (MFN) trade privileges to China subject to annual renewal. Without MFN status, China's exports to the United States would face extraordinarily high tariffs. In 1980 the United States supported China's entry into the World Bank, thus allowing Beijing to obtain loans and grants for economic development. Sino-American cultural ties also expanded rapidly, including mutual exchanges of students and scholars.[11]

Nevertheless, the Taiwan issue re-emerged as the main irritant in Sino-American relations. Despite its pledge on a one-year moratorium, the Carter administration had not completely stopped the flow of US arms to Taiwan, as previous official contracts were fulfilled and private commercial sales continued. In June 1980, it authorized two American aircraft manufacturers to begin negotiations with Taiwan over the possible sale of an advanced fighter called the FX. In 1981, Sino-American relations lost their momentum with the inauguration of Republican President Ronald Reagan, who pursued a programme of massive US military build-up to reverse the strategic balance *vis-à-vis* the Soviet Union. Reagan was inclined to upgrade US relations with Taiwan, either by re-establishing official contacts or by increasing US arms sales. By late 1981, Deng decided that it was time to raise the arms sales issue with the Reagan administration, not only to prevent the sale of the FX to Taipei but also to renegotiate more restrictive guidelines for the future supply of all American weapons to the island.[12]

In October, when meeting with Reagan on the occasion of the North–South Summit at Cancun, Mexico, Premier Zhao Ziyang brought up the arms sales issue. Referring to Beijing's new nine-point plan for peaceful reunification, Zhao said that Taiwan would be offered substantial autonomy under China's sovereignty, thus making it unnecessary and inappropriate for Washington to continue arms sales to Taiwan. China demanded that the United States should pledge not to exceed, in both quality and quantity, the level of arms sales under the Carter administration, agree to gradually reduce arms sales, and set a timetable for their complete termination. However, America wanted China to make a statement on renunciation of forces against Taiwan if further arms sales were to be stopped. The negotiations soon reached a deadlock.

It was not until August 1982 that China and America reached an agreement through reciprocal concessions. While refusing to commit to a firm timetable for ending arms sales, the Reagan administration accepted most of the other Chinese demands and reassured Beijing that the United States had no intention of selling arms to Taiwan forever. The Chinese government believed that a compromise solution was preferable to unregulated US arms sales to Taiwan. According to the

US–China Joint Communiqué on US Arms Sales to Taiwan, signed on 17 August, the United States 'does not seek to carry out a long-term policy of arms sales to Taiwan' and 'intends to reduce gradually its sales of arms to Taiwan, leading over a period of time to a final resolution'. In a unilateral statement issued on the same day, the Chinese Foreign Ministry reiterated its 'fundamental policy of striving for peaceful reunification of the motherland', but it added that, on the Taiwan question, 'which is purely China's internal affair, no misinterpretation or foreign interference is permissible'.[13]

Independent foreign policy and Chinese nationalism

The immediate crisis over US arms sales to Taiwan thus ended, but not China's concerns about the issue of national sovereignty and independence. Shortly after the conclusion of the US–China Joint Communiqué, on 1 September Deng and General Secretary Hua Yaobang declared that China would pursue an 'independent foreign policy'. Beijing's perception of the changing strategic balance between the Soviet Union and the United States was a key factor behind the shift from an overt tilt towards America to an equal-distance approach towards the two superpowers. By 1982, the Soviet Union, under the ailing Brezhnev, had been bogged down in the seeming unwinnable war in Afghanistan. Together with Moscow's support for Vietnam in Cambodia and Cuba in Angola, the Soviet economy appeared to be in serious trouble. On the other hand, the United States under Reagan had regained the upper hand in the struggle for global hegemony. Its massive military build-up (including the ambitious Strategic Defence Initiative), its strong response to the imposition of martial law in Poland in 1981, and the Reagan Doctrine that challenged Marxist regimes in developing countries were all signs of American hegemony under the Reagan administration.[14]

Significantly, the proclamation of 'independent foreign policy' also had to do with the Chinese leaders' nationalist sensitivities at the critical juncture of 1982. The arms sales controversy underscored that, despite normalization, the United States still posed a potential threat to China's sovereignty claims by strengthening Taiwan's military capability to resist the pressure for reunification from Beijing. In coming to this view, Deng, Premier Zhao Ziyang, and other CCP leaders were informed by a group of 'America watchers' serving in research institutes under the State Council's jurisdiction, universities, and the media. In an article published in the US journal *Foreign Affairs* in late 1981, Huan Xiang, a veteran diplomat who served in the Centre for International Studies, dismissed the 'reasons' offered by Washington for continued arms sales to Taiwan, arguing instead that 'there probably is a basic guideline among a number of Americans, that is, to obstruct China's reunification, to keep Taiwan in the US sphere of influence and to use it to hold China in check'. After the conclusion of the 1982 US–China Joint Communiqué, the 'America watchers' of the *People's Daily* warned that although the communiqué 'has broken the deadlock between the two countries', 'this does not mean that the problem has been completely solved ... [T]he fundamental obstacle to the development of Sino-American relations is the U.S. "Taiwan Relations Act"'.[15]

As China was undergoing significant transformation in terms of its socialist economy and relations with the capitalist world, the Communist ideology had lost its appeal, and Chinese nationalism became an increasingly important tool for Deng to legitimize his policy and authority. On 1 September, the Twelfth Party Congress formally enunciated China's 'independent foreign policy'. In his opening speech, Deng talked at great length about the fundamental principle of 'independence and self-reliance': 'While the Chinese people value their friendship and cooperation with other countries and other peoples, they value even more their hard-won independence and sovereign rights.' 'We shall unswervingly follow a policy of opening to the outside world,' Deng continued, but the government should ensure that '[w]e, the Chinese people, have our national self-respect and pride'. Deng identified 'three major tasks' of China during the 1980s, namely 'to accelerate socialist modernization, to strive for China's reunification and particularly for the return of Taiwan to the motherland, and to oppose hegemony and work to safeguard world peace'.[16]

In 1982 national unification with Taiwan was high on the agenda of the CCP leadership. Since the late 1970s, Beijing had changed the basic thrust of its Taiwan policy, from the confrontational approach towards 'liberating' Taiwan to an emphasis on peaceful reunification through negotiation. Thus, China stopped the twenty-year-long bombardment of the offshore islands and called for discussions with the GMD over national unification. In his 'message to compatriots in Taiwan' on 1 January 1979, Marshall Ye Jianying, the chairman of the Standing Committee of the Fifth NPC, enunciated 'nine principles' governing China's Taiwan policy (commonly known as Ye's 'Nine Points'). The most important principle was the formula of 'one country, two systems': Taiwan would be permitted to retain its existing political, economic, and military systems in return for recognition of China's sovereignty over Taiwan. Ye's message called for the opening of reunification talks between representatives of the CCP and the GMD as soon as possible, and the establishment of the so-called three links – direct mail, trade and shipping, and air services – among the Chinese peoples across the Taiwan Strait in preparation for a smooth reunification. While favouring peaceful reunification, Beijing did not renounce the right to use military force against Taiwan if necessary. It must be emphasized that, although the 'nine principles' were delivered in Ye's name, Deng was the chief architect of China's Taiwan policy, particularly the concept of 'one country, two systems'.[17]

But it was Hong Kong rather than Taiwan that first saw the application of Deng's 'one country, two systems' formula. On 22 September, shortly after Deng's announcement of China's 'independent foreign policy', British Prime Minister Margaret Thatcher arrived in Beijing to discuss the future of Hong Kong. Indeed, Deng and his colleagues had not intended to discuss Hong Kong's retrocession before the resolution of the Taiwan question. But due to the initiative by Hong Kong Governor Murray MacLehose in raising the immediate issue of the 99-year lease of the New Territories (which would expire by 1997) in March 1979, the Chinese leaders decided to recover Hong Kong and thus set a precedent for Taiwan's reunification.

Britain aimed to retain its sovereignty over Hong Kong Island and the Kowloon Peninsula, which were ceded in perpetuity by treaties, and failing that, to insist on continued British administration over these territories after 1997, while recognizing China's sovereignty over Hong Kong. When meeting with Deng on 24 September, Thatcher said that if China sought to recover the whole of Hong Kong, it would have adverse economic consequences on the territory, which would in turn affect China's economic modernization. In response, Deng asserted: 'On the question of sovereignty, China has no room for manoeuvre. To be frank, the question is not open to discussion … China will recover [the whole of] Hong Kong in 1997.' Rejecting Thatcher's hint about British administration in exchange for Chinese sovereignty, Deng said that the 'one country, two systems' model would allow Hong Kong to maintain its economic prosperity and capitalist way of life after 1997.[18]

During the Sino-British negotiations over Hong Kong between 1982 and 1984, China was unyielding on the principle of full sovereignty. At last, Britain had to make all the compromises, conceding both sovereignty and administration to China. On 19 December 1984, Thatcher and Zhao signed the Sino-British Joint Declaration, stipulating China's resumption of sovereignty over Hong Kong on 1 July 1997.[19] On 13 April 1987, China also concluded a joint declaration with Portugal concerning the return of Macao to the motherland in 1999.

In the 1980s, nationalism also shaped China's relations with two of its Asian neighbours, Japan and Vietnam. Since the establishment of diplomatic relations in 1972 and the conclusion of a peace treaty in 1978, Sino-Japanese ties had grown amicably, especially in the economic sphere. Nevertheless, there were unresolved issues between the two countries, notably the dispute over the Diaoyu Islands and the question of Japan's war responsibility. In 1982, a history textbook issue emerged as an irritant in their relationship. The new Japanese textbooks, approved by the Ministry of Education, referred to Japan's aggression in China since 1931 as 'entering China'. To Chinese nationalists, however, it was a complete distortion of historical facts and open glorification of Japanese militarism. Anti-Japanese feeling in China exploded three years later. On 18 September 1985, the date marking the outbreak of the 1931 Mukden Incident and the fortieth anniversary of the end of the Sino-Japanese War, several hundred university students in Beijing staged large-scale demonstrations against the Japanese. The anti-Japanese demonstrations spread to other Chinese cities such as Xi'an and Chengdu, where the students chanted 'boycott Japanese goods' and stoned Japanese cars.[20]

Besides the history issue, the Chinese demonstrators were also angry about what they saw as Japan's 'second invasion' of China in the age of economic opening-up. They resented the grossly disproportionate importance of Sino-Japanese trade to the two economies: while Japan was China's leading trading partner, China only made up a fraction of Japan's total trade. And there was the negative perception of allegedly 'cunning' Japanese merchants and Japan's refusal to open its markets. But beneath genuine anti-Japanese sentiment, the Chinese students were increasingly disillusioned with their own government. By 1985, half a decade of economic reform had brought about pressing problems such as corruption, bureaucracy, and inequality. Thus, the students demonstrated in the name of nationalism to embarrass the regime. Realizing the importance of Japan's investment and technology transfer, the Chinese government prevented the escalation of anti-Japanese ferment through a mix of persuasion and suppression.

If Sino-Japanese friction in 1985 resulted from the growth of Chinese popular nationalism, the Sino-Vietnamese conflict in the South China Sea in 1988 was due mainly to the Chinese government's pursuit of national greatness. On 14 March, the Chinese and Vietnamese naval forces clashed on Johnson Reef in the Spratly Islands, the collective name of over 200 small islands, rocks and reefs scattered west of the Philippines and north of Borneo. Potentially rich in maritime resources such as natural gas and oil, the Spratlys were claimed by not only

China, Taiwan, and Vietnam, but also the Philippines, Malaysia, and Brunei. While other claimants had all occupied some of the disputed islands, China did not seek to establish a permanent physical presence in the area until 1988. The decision to use force against Vietnam over Johnson Reef could be attributed to China's growing naval power, Beijing's calculations of minimum adverse international reaction (due to Vietnam's invasion of Cambodia), and the bureaucratic interests of the PLA Navy to compete for budgetary resources. After occupying six coral reefs, the PLA Navy did not evict the Vietnamese from other parts of the archipelago. The Spratlys campaign demonstrated China's determination to assert sovereignty claims over disputed territories.[21]

Sino-Soviet normalization

To secure a peaceful international environment for China's domestic reconstruction, as early as 1979 Deng began to ponder the prospect of Sino-Soviet normalization. In April, China made its first overture to the Soviets, informing them of the decision not to renew the 1950 Sino-Soviet Treaty and proposing the holding of normalization talks. The talks at vice-ministerial level took place in November and ended without agreement. After the Soviet invasion of Afghanistan in December, Beijing postponed the scheduled second-round meeting. Despite the lack of progress on political relations, bilateral trade and cultural contacts between China and the Soviet Union expanded. By 1982, as the strategic international balance of power was perceived to have shifted to the advantage of the United States, China gained a new incentive to improve relations with Moscow.[22]

To Deng, there were three obstacles to normalization that needed to be addressed, namely Soviet troop withdrawal from Mongolia and the Sino-Soviet border, Soviet withdrawal from Afghanistan, and Vietnamese withdrawal from Cambodia. After the accession to power of Mikhail Gorbachev, in April 1985, Deng hinted that if Moscow found it difficult to remove the three obstacles simultaneously, it could start with the Vietnamese withdrawal from Cambodia. In October, Deng proposed to Gorbachev, via the Romanian leader, his willingness to travel to Moscow for discussions if the Soviet Union agreed to exert pressure on Hanoi regarding Cambodia. In July 1986, Gorbachev responded with his famous Vladivostok speech. Accordingly, he made a number of proposals and suggested Moscow's willingness to discuss with Beijing 'any issue' 'at any time'.

Sino-Soviet border talks resumed in February 1987. By October 1988, the two sides had reached an agreement on the eastern section of the border (except for Bear Island), and agreed to begin discussion about the western section. In early 1987, Moscow announced its intention to withdraw some units from Mongolia later that year. Progress was also made on the Afghanistan front: in April 1988, under UN mediation, the concerned parties signed the Geneva Accord, stipulating the beginning of Soviet military withdrawal in May and its completion in nine months' time. In December, Gorbachev announced at the UN that Moscow would reduce Soviet forces by 500,000 men in two years, including 260,000 troops stationed in Central Asia and the Far East. Also that month, Vietnam announced its intention to remove 18,000 troops from Cambodia. In April 1989, Hanoi committed itself to a complete military withdrawal by the end of September. Thus, the three obstacles to normalization were removed one by one, paving the way for the historic summit between Deng and Gorbachev, scheduled for 15–18 May.

Nevertheless, by the time Gorbachev landed in Beijing, a student revolution was in the making, so that some of his programmed activities including the formal welcome ceremony had to be rescheduled. After a decade of economic reforms, rampant corruption, soaring prices, growing social inequalities, and the lack of political reform had plagued the CCP into a profound legitimacy crisis in the eyes of the Chinese people, particularly the younger generation. The tension between state and society had had its first public manifestation in late 1986, when university students at several major cities held demonstrations for political reform and against corruption. It contributed to the downfall of General Secretary Hu Yaobang, who was criticized as being too soft in dealing with 'bourgeois liberalization'. After Hu died on 15 April, students gathered at Tiananmen Square in large numbers in commemoration of their beloved liberal reformer. The commemorative gathering soon developed into massive demonstrations in Beijing and other major cities, hunger strikes, and demands for political reform and dialogue with top leaders. On 20 May, martial law was declared in Beijing. The CCP leadership was split over how to respond to the student protests, with General Secretary Zhao Ziyang (who succeeded Hu) advocating reconciliation while Premier Li Peng and other conservatives called for hard-line suppression. Finally, the conservatives won Deng over, and the 'ultimate decision-maker' in China (Zhao had revealed this secret 1987 Party resolution's decision to Gorbachev in May) decided to use military means to end the 'great turmoil'.[23] On 3–4 June, PLA soldiers fought their way into Tiananmen Square, killing an unknown number of students and other Beijing residents.

The Deng–Gorbachev summit was overshadowed by the student demonstrations. Nonetheless, Sino-Soviet relations were normalized.

After Tiananmen, Deng was confronted with new enemies and new challenges on the domestic and international fronts.

Alignment with America or national independence?

Since 1979 Deng had been pursuing a pragmatic foreign policy. With economic development as the major domestic task, China needed a peaceful international environment. After the establishment of full diplomatic relations in 1979, China and the United States expanded their cooperation at all levels. By 1982, perceiving that the strategic balance of power had shifted in America's favour, Deng declared an 'independent foreign policy' whereby China would adjust its overt pro-America tilt by pursuing an even-handed approach towards the two superpowers. Nonetheless, as Robert Ross wrote: 'Except in propaganda, China never implemented its "independent foreign policy." Rather, during the remaining years of the 1980s, across a wide range of issues, China moved significantly closer to the United States, seeking and developing unprecedented US–PRC strategic, economic, and cultural cooperation.'[24]

While it is true that China continued to forge much closer relations with America than with the Soviet Union, the proclamation of 'independent foreign policy' in 1982 was also related to Deng's nationalist concerns at this particular juncture. In the 1980s, national reunification with Taiwan and Hong Kong was high on the agenda of Deng's government. With the gradual weakening of the Communist ideology in the age of unprecedented economic reform, Deng appealed to nationalism as a legitimizing force. Despite growing economic and diplomatic ties with America, China adhered to its identity as an independent state on the world stage, determined to maintain its national sovereignty and territorial integrity.

Notes

1 Lu Ning, *The Dynamics of Foreign Policy Decision-Making in China* (Boulder: Westview Press, 1997), 156–9, 162.

2 Immanuel C. Y. Hsü, *China Without Mao: The Search for a New Order*, 2nd edition (New York: Oxford University Press, 1990), 92–107, 168.

3 Editorial Committee for Party Literature, CCP Central Committee (ed.), *Selected Works of Deng Xiaoping*, vol. iii: *1982–1992* (Beijing: Foreign Languages Press, 1994), 119.

4 Madelyn C. Ross, 'China's International Economic Behaviour', in Thomas W. Robinson and David Shambaugh (eds), *Chinese Foreign Policy: Theory and Practice* (Oxford: Clarendon Press, 1995), 436, 443.

5 Robert Ross, *Negotiating Cooperation: The United States and China, 1969–1989* (Stanford: Stanford University Press, 1995), 274.

6 Harry Harding, *A Fragile Relationship: The United States and China since 1972* (Washington, D.C.: The Brookings Institution, 1992), 86–7.
7 James Mann, *About Face: A History of America's Curious Relationship with China, from Nixon to Clinton* (New York: Alfred A. Knopf, 1999), 97–8.
8 Ibid., 99.
9 See Xiaoming Zhang, 'China's 1979 War with Vietnam: A Reassessment', *CQ* 184 (December 2005): 851–74.
10 Harding, op. cit., 87–94.
11 Mann, op. cit., 104–9.
12 See Harding, op. cit., 112–19.
13 Ibid., 383–8.
14 Ibid., 121–4.
15 David Shambaugh, *Beautiful Imperialist: China Perceives America, 1972–1990* (Princeton, N.J.: Princeton University Press, 1991), 261, 265.
16 *Selected Works of Deng Xiaoping,* vol. iii, 13–16.
17 Michael D. Swaine, 'Chinese Decision-Making Regarding Taiwan, 1979–2000', in David M. Lampton (ed.), *The Making of Chinese Foreign and Security Policy in the Era of Reform* (Stanford: Stanford University Press, 2001), 310–13.
18 *Selected Works of Deng Xiaoping,* vol. iii, 23–5.
19 See Steve Tsang, *A Modern History of Hong Kong* (Hong Kong: Hong Kong University Press, 2004), 218–27.
20 My account draws on Allen S. Whiting, *China Eyes Japan* (Berkeley: University of California Press, 1989).
21 See John W. Garver, 'China's Push Through the South China Sea: The Interaction of Bureaucratic and National Interests', *CQ* 132 (December 1992): 999–1028; M. Taylor Fravel, *Strong Borders, Secure Nation: Cooperation and Conflict in China's Territorial Disputes* (Princeton: Princeton University Press, 2008), 287–8, 294–6.
22 This section is based on Chi Su, 'The Strategic Triangle and China's Soviet Policy', in Robert S. Ross (ed.), *China, the United States, and the Soviet Union: Tripolarity and Policy Making in the Cold War* (Armonk: M. E. Sharpe, 1993), 48–56.
23 In his recorded recollections, Zhao revealed the deep division within the Party and how his revelation of Deng's paramount role in decision-making had been misunderstood by others including Deng himself. See Zhao Ziyang, *Prisoner of the State: The Secret Journal of Zhao Ziyang* (London: Simon & Schuster, 2009), 3–7, 15–24, 45–9.
24 Ross, *Negotiating Cooperation,* 214.

9 Post-Cold War challenges and multilateral diplomacy, 1990s

After the 1989 Tiananmen crackdown, the CCP leadership faced tremendous domestic and international challenges. China was isolated by America, Japan, and Western European countries, at least initially. The collapse of socialism in Eastern Europe and the Soviet Union sent more shock waves through the Chinese capital, setting off debates about the future of reform and China's relations with the outside world. Under a siege mentality, the Chinese leaders responded to the growing pro-independence trend in Taiwan by conducting military exercises in the Taiwan Strait in 1995–6, thereby precipitating a crisis with America. By the late 1990s, the Chinese government finally overcame the post-Tiananmen Sino-American estrangement and affirmed China's identity as a responsible state in the post-Cold War international system.

The collapse of communism

Because of his sympathetic attitude towards the student protests in 1989, General Secretary Zhao Ziyang was ousted from office by Deng Xiaoping. Replacing Zhao was Jiang Zemin, the former Party chief of Shanghai who had earned Deng's praise by his firm suppression of the protests in the city. Although Deng was still the paramount leader, the post-Tiananmen nuclear circle that surrounded him now consisted of Jiang, Li Peng, Yang Shangkun, and Chen Yun.[1] With his authority and prestige weakened, Deng could no longer dominate the policy agenda. The conservatives such as Chen Yun became more assertive in decision-making. Blaming the 'student turmoil' on Deng's market reform, the conservatives sought to restore some degree of central planning to the economy and implement an austerity programme. In the last few months of 1989, the Communist regimes in Eastern Europe collapsed one after another, to be replaced by multi-party parliamentary democracies. The crisis of socialism in Eastern Europe provoked debate within the CCP about the future of reform in China. To the conservatives, the changes reflected the 'peaceful evolution' of socialist countries towards capitalism inspired by hostile Western forces.[2]

As the political crisis in Eastern Europe unfolded, Deng gave his views on the international situation to leading members of the CCP Central Committee on 4 September. Deng thought China should 'observe the situation coolly' and 'act calmly', and should not be 'impatient'. As it was difficult to predict how far the 'upheavals' in Eastern Europe would go, China should observe the developments coolly. Concerning the capitalist countries, China should 'maintain vigilance' and 'keep them as friends but also have a clear understanding of what they are doing'. Meanwhile, China should keep a low profile and 'quietly immerse [itself] in practical work to accomplish something'. While the Eastern European countries were 'in turmoil', argued Deng, China should make its socialist system a 'success' through economic modernization: 'if China holds its ground and attains its goals for development, that will demonstrate the superiority of socialism.'[3] Deng's advice, best summarized in the eight characters *taoguang yanghui* (keep a low profile and bide time), *yousuo zuowei* (accomplish things where possible), guided China through the challenges of the post-Cold War environment.

It was the slow death of the Soviet Union between 1990 and 1991 that really shocked China. During the 1989 summit, Gorbachev and Deng had pledged to develop Sino-Soviet relations on the basis of mutual equality and non-interference in each other's internal affairs. Publicly, Beijing put on a brave face by declaring that what happened in the Soviet Union was the choice of its own people. In internal debate, though, the Chinese leaders condemned Gorbachev as a 'traitor' to communism. The CCP endeavoured to influence events in the Soviet Union by lending support to the hard-liners within the CPSU, for example top-level Party exchanges and the offer of commercial credits to the beleaguered Soviet economy.[4]

But the balance of power between the CPSU hard-liners and the anti-communist force in the Soviet Union increasingly shifted in the latter's favour. In June 1991, Boris Yeltsin, a Russian nationalist who broke away from the CPSU, was elected President of the Russian Federation. On 19 August, a day before the official signing of a new union treaty that would delegate more power to the Soviet republics, the hard-liners staged a coup in Moscow and house-arrested Gorbachev, who was then on vacation in the Crimea. Apparently with foreknowledge of the hard-liners' plot, Beijing gave detailed coverage of the events in the official media. In private, the Politburo formulated a directive to guide lower-level cadres, praising the downfall of Gorbachev and recommending recognition of the State Emergency Committee. As a result of Yeltsin's firm resistance and the lack of popular support, however, the hard-liners' coup collapsed in a matter of days.

After the failed coup, Gorbachev resumed power as President of the Soviet Union (but resigned as CPSU General Secretary). But Gorbachev was now a leader in name only. On 8 December, Yeltsin and the leaders of Ukraine and Belarus, declaring that the Soviet Union was no longer in existence, announced the establishment of the Commonwealth of Independent States, which was open to the other republics to join. On 25 December, Gorbachev resigned from the presidency, symbolizing the official demise of the Soviet Union.

With the collapse of Soviet communism, China had no choice but to deal with Russia and other former Soviet republics on a normal state-to-state basis. In line with Deng's guidance, China would continue its path to building socialism with Chinese characteristics. As Foreign Minister Qian Qichen put it, China and Russia would develop 'a friendly neighbor relationship free of ideology'.[5] On 27 December, Qian formally informed Yeltsin of the Chinese decision to recognize the Russian Federation. Beijing also moved quickly to recognize all the former Soviet republics.

Post-Tiananmen Sino-American relations

The 1989 Tiananmen massacre shocked the American public. On 5 and 20 June, President George H. W. Bush announced the imposition of sanctions on China, including suspension of high-level political exchanges, military cooperation and arms sales, and the postponement of loans from international financial agencies. US allies such as Japan and the European Community followed suit. Nevertheless, due to his personal attachment to China (where he had served as the chief of the US Liaison Office in Beijing 14 years earlier) and the need for China's cooperation over other policy issues such as Cambodia, Bush wanted to maintain a direct and personal channel of communication with top Chinese leaders. Shortly after the imposition of sanctions, on 20 June Bush sent a personal letter to Deng, explaining that the decision resulted from Congressional pressure and the American public. In early July, the President himself violated the ban on high-level contacts by asking National Security Advisor Brent Scowcroft and Deputy Secretary of State Lawrence Eagleburger to make a secret trip to Beijing to explain the difficulties faced by the administration regarding sanctions. In December, the two presidential special envoys again secretly visited China to meet the Chinese leaders.[6]

Deng, too, faced his own difficulties. After Tiananmen, the paramount leader was put on the defensive by the Party conservatives. The political earthquake in Eastern Europe in late 1989 underscored the danger of 'peaceful evolution' inspired by hostile Western forces. Deng blamed Washington for the current crisis in Sino-American relations, arguing: 'It is up to the person who tied the knot to untie it.'[7] In other words, the United States should take the initiative to end the sanctions on China if bilateral relations were to return to normality. On the other hand, Deng realized that, in order to regain the initiative in economic policy-making at home, he needed to end the American-led Western sanctions and China's international isolation as soon as possible. To allow Sino-American relations to spiral downwards would only play into the hands of the conservatives who opposed China's opening to the capitalist world.

To break the multilateral sanctions, China exploited the contradictions within the Western camp. Because of its economic links with China, Japan had been a reluctant follower of Washington's sanction regime. As early as October 1989 Japan had advocated the resumption of small-scale World Bank loans to China. At the G7 summit in July 1990, Japan announced the resumption of development loans to China. The ban on high-level contacts, too, melted away due to the European eagerness to trade with China. In September 1990, Qian Qichen, attending the UN General Assembly meeting in New York, met with the three foreign ministers of the European Commission – Italy, Luxembourg, and Ireland. In October the following year, the European Community decided to gradually resume bilateral relations with China.[8]

The Iraqi invasion of Kuwait in the summer of 1990 provided an incentive for Washington to improve relations with China. In early November, Secretary of State James Baker met his Chinese counterpart in Cairo during his Middle East tour. Baker told Qian that, in return for Beijing's promise not to obstruct the passage of any resolution by the UN Security Council authorizing the use of all necessary means against Iraq, the administration would be prepared to lift the sanctions on China in the near future, and would not oppose the provision of a World Bank loan (worth US$100 million) to China. When the Security Council voted on a resolution authorizing the use of force against Iraq in late November, China made no attempt to block it.

By the autumn of 1991, the US administration was willing to lift the sanctions on China. Now that the Gulf War had ended with the defeat of Iraq, the United States deepened its involvement in the Middle East. The deteriorating situation in the Soviet Union after the aborted August coup also commanded Washington's attention. On 15 November,

Secretary Baker made the first US official visit to Beijing since Tiananmen. Baker proposed that Washington would gradually lift the sanctions on US exports and high-level contacts, and would support China's bid to join the General Agreement on Tariffs and Trade (GATT). But he added that America in turn needed China's cooperation over other issues, such as improvements in human rights at home and prevention of arms proliferation overseas. Praising the proposed lifting of US sanctions, Qian pledged to improve China's protection of intellectual property rights but insisted that the issue of human rights should not be used as an excuse for foreign interference in China's internal affairs. Nevertheless, Baker's visit marked the beginning of the end of US sanctions on China.[9]

But the spectre of Tiananmen did not go away. The issue of China's human rights was brought to the fore by the new Clinton administration, inaugurated in 1993. With the US economy as his priority, Clinton was determined to build consensus with Congress, not least to ensure the passage of future budget and health care reform bills.[10] The first issue of China policy that he needed to work with Congress was the possible extension of China's MFN trading status for 1994.

From the outset, the MFN debate was bound up with concerns about China's human rights abuses. In the aftermath of Tiananmen, China had made some efforts to engage with American and Western criticisms of its human rights record, for example, by producing the White Paper on the subject in October 1991 and receiving human rights delegations from foreign countries. Nevertheless, Beijing emphasized rights to subsistence and development, while attacking America's own human rights record regarding police brutality and racial discrimination at home.[11]

The American government and society were divided over the MFN issue. The Commerce and Treasury Departments, trade-related committees of Congress, and business corporations lobbied for MFN extension, while the State Department, anti-communist members of Congress, and human rights groups opposed it. After weighing both sides of the argument, on 28 May 1993, Clinton issued an executive order linking MFN extension to improvements in China's human rights record. China ought to satisfy the pre-existing requirements of US law about emigration and prison labour exports, and demonstrate 'overall, significant progress' in such areas as release of political dissidents and humane treatment of prisoners.[12]

Aware of divided opinion within American society, China did not hesitate to exploit it to its own advantage through the lure of trade. Significantly, by 1993 China's economy took off again after two years of the conservative-insisted austerity economic programme. This was largely due to Deng's high-profile visit to Shenzhen and the Zhuhai SEZ in early 1992, where he openly talked about the importance of reform and bluntly attacked the 'left' as the main danger to the Party. After Deng's southern tour, economic reform was once again high on the agenda of the Chinese government. In October, the Fourteenth Party Congress endorsed the creation of a 'socialist market economy' as the main goal of reform.[13]

With an impressive growth rate of 13 per cent in 1993, China was confident that it could demonstrate to Washington the potential economic costs of linking MFN with human rights. In November 1993, German Chancellor Helmut Kohl accompanied by a huge entourage of businessmen arrived in China, and departed with signed trade contracts worth several billion German marks. This was the same as for France after the visit by the French Minister of Foreign Trade and Jiang Zemin's return visit in 1994. China, moreover, exerted pressure on America directly. In April 1994, it sent a trade mission to the United States, hinting at the prospect of purchasing more American goods if Sino-American relations improved. On the other hand, prior to his visit to China, the Chinese played tough with the US Secretary of State by detaining a dozen dissidents including Wei Jingsheng (an activist of the 1978 'Democracy Wall' movement) and Wang Dan (a student leader of the 1989 Tiananmen demonstrations). Against this background, Clinton made a U-turn over his policy: on 26 May he announced that the United States would 'delink' human rights from the annual extension of MFN status to China.[14]

The MFN/human rights controversy indeed reflected the wider debate over containment or engagement insofar as China policy was concerned. Those who advocated the containment of China pointed to the growing trade imbalance between America and China. During the early 1990s, China's exports to America far exceeded its imports, enjoying, for example, a trade surplus worth US$36,772 million in 1995 alone.[15] The Americans complained of the annual trade deficits, the hidden barriers to entry to the China market, and inadequate protection of intellectual property. Besides, China was criticized for its support for the so-called 'rogue states', such as the sale of missiles to Pakistan and Iran. But it was Taiwan that provided advocates of containment with ammunition in the mid-1990s.

Chinese nationalism, Taiwan, and Japan

At the Fourteenth Party Congress in late 1992, Jiang Zemin consolidated his position as the nucleus of the third generation leadership.

But lacking the revolutionary legitimacy and authority of Mao and Deng, Jiang was cautious and consultative in decision-making. His domestic priority was the maintenance of political and social stability. Diplomatically, Jiang basically followed Deng's 'independent foreign policy line', with national reunification with Taiwan as one of his main preoccupations.[16]

By the middle of the 1990s, however, the prospect of unification had become more remote than ever. Since the beginning of gradual democratization in the late 1980s, the pro-independence political force in Taiwan had been growing in strength. In 1988, the Taiwan-born Lee Teng-hui became President. Using economic assistance as leverage, Lee pursued 'pragmatic diplomacy' towards small and poor developing countries in order to secure their diplomatic recognition of Taiwan. He also undertook a campaign to join the UN as a separate political entity. Despite growing economic ties between China and Taiwan, Taipei gave a lukewarm response to Beijing's 'one country, two systems' model for national reunification, and instead insisted on the 'three nos' – no (direct) contact, no negotiation, and no compromise with China.

In January 1995, Jiang promulgated a major eight-point initiative, or the 'Jiang Eight Points'. Drawing on the core principles of Deng's 'one country, two systems' formula, the Jiang Eight Points proposed a phased process of rapprochement and negotiations on an equal footing leading to reunification. Beijing would be prepared to address all of Taiwan's concerns as long as Taiwan accepted the principle of 'one China' and established direct links with the mainland.[17]

Lee, however, counter-proposed that China should renounce the use of force against Taiwan before the start of any negotiations. In Beijing's opinion, Lee had no intention of national reunification. Cross-Strait relations took a sharp turn for the worse in May, when the Clinton administration, under Congressional pressure, decided to permit Lee to make a 'private' visit to his alma mater, Cornell University. During his stay in America, Lee made a number of what Beijing saw as 'provocative' speeches, such as repeatedly using the term 'Republic of China on Taiwan'. By allowing Lee's visit and supporting Taiwan generally, Beijing suspected, America actually aimed to 'keep China off-balance'.[18] To halt Taiwan's drift towards *de facto* independence and to send a strong message to Washington, Jiang, in consultation with the civilian and military leadership, resorted to coercive diplomacy in the Taiwan Strait. In view of the Taiwanese legislative elections in December 1995 and the presidential election in March 1996, China launched a series of naval exercises in August and November 1995, as well as missile tests in July 1995 and March 1996. In response to China's military actions in early 1996, the Clinton administration deployed two US aircraft carrier battle groups in the vicinity of Taiwan to stabilize the situation. Taiwan's first direct presidential election saw the victory of Lee Teng-hui earning 54 per cent of the vote. Although China's coercive diplomacy had apparently scared off many pro-independence voters, it also contributed to the crushing defeat of the two pro-reunification candidates.

With the relaxation of tension after the Taiwan elections, the Jiang government came to realize that the only effective way to deter Taiwan was to persuade Washington not to encourage or support any pro-independence initiatives. China wanted America to reaffirm its commitment to a 'one China' policy. The Clinton administration, for its part, also wanted to re-establish a strategic consensus on developing Sino-American relations. All this paved the way for the Jiang–Clinton summit meetings in 1997 and 1998 (see below).

It is important to mention other manifestations of Chinese aggressive nationalism in the mid-1990s. In 1990 and 1996, the Chinese nationalists directed their anger at what they saw as the Japanese infringement of China's sovereignty over the Diaoyu Islands (or the Senkaku Islands in Japanese). An uninhabited archipelago of eight desolate rocks lying in the East China Sea between Taiwan and Okinawa, the Diaoyu were potentially rich in natural gas and oil reserves. They were claimed by China (based on historical records dating back to the Ming dynasty) and Taiwan, as well as Japan (based on the 1895 Sino-Japanese Treaty, which ceded Taiwan to Japan, and the US return of Okinawa and the 'administrative rights' over the islands to Japan in 1972). When establishing diplomatic relations in 1972 and concluding a peace treaty in 1978, Beijing and Tokyo agreed to put aside the islands' sovereignty issue. However, in September 1990 Japan reportedly decided to recognize a lighthouse on the main Diaoyu Island, previously erected by a right-wing group. It triggered off Beijing's diplomatic protest and anti-Japanese demonstrations in Taiwan, Hong Kong, and the United States.

In the summer of 1996, Japanese right-wingers erected another lighthouse on the islands. After Japan openly reasserted its sovereignty claims, in September anti-Japanese demonstrations erupted in Taiwan, Hong Kong, and mainland China. Nationalist sentiment ran so high that the Hong Kong Chinese attempted to land on one of the islands, which resulted in one of them being drowned. The Chinese government was confronted with a dilemma. On the one hand, it felt obligated to champion the nationalist cause, not least for the sake of propping up the CCP's legitimacy after the Tiananmen crackdown and the collapse of Soviet communism. On the other, Beijing worried that excessive popular nationalism among mainland Chinese would adversely affect Sino-Japanese economic relations and domestic stability. Consequently, the Chinese government responded with a two-pronged strategy – suppressing 'unauthorized' mass protests in China while taking a firm stance on sovereignty in official propaganda.[19]

In 1996 the growth of Chinese popular nationalism was also manifested in the publication of *China Can Say No* by five young Chinese ultra-nationalists, which quickly became a commercial bestseller. Disillusioned with US policy, such as its support for Taiwan and its alleged opposition to China's bids for GATT entry and the 2000 Olympic Games, the authors argued that China (or more precisely, the Chinese government) should feel confident and competent enough to stand up against the arrogant superpower.[20]

Multilateralism and globalization

China's policy regarding Taiwan and the Diaoyu Islands contributed to the proliferation of the 'China threat' theories in the Western academic and official circles during the 1990s. Seeing China as authoritarian, war-prone, and anti-status quo, the protagonists of the theories based their cases on cultural, economic, and military grounds. In 1993, Harvard political scientist Samuel Huntington put forward the 'clash of civilizations' thesis, portraying Confucian China as a threat to Western civilization. Others warned that a 'Greater China' superpower was in the making, as a result of the growing economic integration of coastal China, Hong Kong, Taiwan, and the Overseas Chinese communities in Asia. From a geopolitical perspective, China's coercive diplomacy against Taiwan, its regional rivalry with Japan and India, and its challenge to America's global hegemony all demonstrated the danger of China's aggressive nationalism.[21]

To Beijing, the 'China threat' theories were propagated by hostile elements in the West and elsewhere, which aimed to damage China's international reputation (in view of its booming economy), justify the proponents' own national ambitions (such as India's nuclear development), and keep China down (to perpetuate American supremacy). Partly to counter the perception of the 'China threat', in 1997 the Chinese government articulated a 'new security concept'. Unlike the Cold War mentality and old-style military alliances, it claimed, the 'new security concept' was based on mutual trust, peaceful resolution of disputes, and mutually beneficial economic relations.[22] It is no coincidence that the concept was unveiled at a time when Washington and Tokyo were renegotiating new defence guidelines, which provided for a larger defence role for Japan and missile defence arrangements in Asia. By implicitly attacking outmoded Cold War alliances, China obviously had an eye on the reinvigorated US–Japan security alliance and its implications for Taiwan.

Nevertheless, the 'new security concept' also reflected the 'multilateral turn' in China's diplomacy in the latter half of the 1990s. Accordingly, China developed 'constructive strategic partnerships' with America and other powers, engaged with multilateral security and economic institutions in Asia, and endeavoured to join the World Trade Organization (WTO). China embraced multilateralism partly for instrumental reasons: to end its post-Tiananmen international isolation and to increase its influence in the region. But China was also concerned about its international status: it wanted to be recognized as a 'responsible great power' by the international community.[23]

At a personal level, Jiang was obsessed with his place in history. On 19 February 1997, Deng died, marking the end of an era. The holding of the Fifteenth Party Congress later that year completed the transition of power to the third generation leadership centred on Jiang. At midnight on 30 June, Jiang presided over the resumption of Chinese sovereignty over Hong Kong, which Britain had acquired through imperialist wars and 'unequal treaties' one and a half centuries earlier. The retrocession of Hong Kong symbolized the formal end of the 'century of humiliation', and all Chinese, on the mainland and abroad, celebrated it with a sense of national pride. (In 1999 Portuguese Macau was also returned to China.) Nonetheless, realizing that the reunification with Hong Kong and Macau through the 'one country, two systems' formula was primarily Deng's achievement, Jiang was anxious to build his own legacy in China's foreign policy.

Jiang sought Washington's symbolic recognition of his legitimate position and of China's great-power status through summitry. On 28 October 1997, Jiang made his state visit to the United States. In discussions, Jiang promised to stop selling cruise missiles to Iran, while Clinton agreed to allow the sale of civilian technology to China. The summit marked the formal end of the post-Tiananmen Sino-American estrangement. Following Jiang's visit, Beijing released high-profile dissidents such as Wei Jingsheng and Wang Dan, on condition that they would agree to go into exile in America. Washington, in turn, stopped supporting annual resolutions condemning China at the UN Commission on Human Rights. The stage was set for Clinton's return visit to China. On 29 June 1998, in Shanghai Clinton for the first time publicly affirmed the 'three nos': that the United States would not support Taiwan's independence, the creation of 'two Chinas', or Taiwan's admission to the UN. As a result of the two summits, China and America pledged to build a 'constructive strategic partnership'[24]

A new crisis emerged in May 1999, however, when the United States accidentally bombed the Chinese Embassy in Belgrade during the Kosovo conflict, killing Chinese personnel and destroying the compound building. It set off a wave of anti-American protests and attacks on the US Embassy in Beijing by young Chinese nationalists. To the Chinese nationalists and government, the attack was not 'accidental' due to faulty maps, but deliberate with the aim of 'humiliating' China. Nevertheless, after acquiescing in weeks-long anti-US protests, the Chinese government, eager to contain popular nationalism, finally accepted American apologies and compensation and let Sino-American relations move on.[25]

In the latter half of the 1990s, China engaged more actively with the existing multilateral economic and security organizations in the region, notably the Asia-Pacific Economic Cooperation Forum and the Association of Southeast Asian Nations (ASEAN) Regional Forum. It played a key role in establishing a new Asia-only grouping in 1997 – the ASEAN Plus Three comprising China, Japan, South Korea, and the ten ASEAN states. Also in 1997, China and ASEAN signed a joint declaration which renounced the use of force and envisaged joint exploration and development of the disputed islands in the South China Sea. During the 1997–8 Asian financial crisis, China resisted the pressure to devalue its own currency, while offering financial aid to the hardest-hit neighbouring countries. China's response earned the world's admiration.

China took the lead in developing strategic partnerships with Russia and the former Soviet republics. In 1996, during his visit to Beijing, Russian President Boris Yeltsin and Jiang Zemin announced the development of a 'strategic partnership of cooperation' between China and Russia. Also that year, the leaders of China, Russia, Kazakhstan, Kyrgyzstan, and Tajikistan met in Shanghai, agreeing to finalize border settlements and to initiate confidence-building measures in Central Asia. The 'Shanghai Five' security regime, as it became known, would evolve into a formal organization in 2001.

China made efforts to mediate in the nuclear crisis between North Korea and the United States/South Korea. It aimed to achieve a stable, nuclear-free Korean peninsula and ensure the survival of the North Korean communist regime, while allowing China–South Korean economic relations to flourish. In 1994 Beijing helped defuse the first nuclear crisis by facilitating the conclusion of the Agreed Framework between North Korea and America. Accordingly, Washington promised to supply two light-water nuclear reactors and fuel oil to North Korea in return for Pyongyang's suspension of its nuclear weapons programme.

China's acceptance of international norms and regimes went far beyond Asia. China was a signatory to a number of major international agreements, for example, the Comprehensive Test Ban Treaty (1996) and the two International Covenants on Economic, Social, and Cultural Rights (1997) and on Civil and Political Rights (1998). Besides, China participated in an increasing number of UN-sponsored organizations, and made steady progress in compliance with agreements and norms on issues ranging from arms control to North–South relations to environmental protection. Thus, China behaved like 'a satisfied system maintainer' rather than 'a system reformer or system-transforming revolutionary'.[26]

Finally, China fully embraced economic globalization. On 15 November 1999, after protracted negotiations, China and America reached a bilateral agreement on China's accession to the WTO by 2001. After the 1997–8 Asian financial crisis, Jiang and Premier Zhu Rongji had gained a deeper appreciation of economic interdependence, and were more willing to make major concessions to America that would facilitate China's full integration into the global economy.

Nationalism or multilateralism?

In the course of the 1990s, the main thrust of China's diplomacy changed from a passive response to the post-Tiananmen and post-Cold War challenges to a proactive approach towards embracing multilateralism and globalization. As Michael Yahuda argues, '1995 may be seen as an important turning point marking the time when Chinese diplomacy became more active, as opposed to being for the most part reactive to the initiatives of others.' While identifying 1997–8 as the timing of the shift, Robert Sutter similarly notes: 'The Asian financial crisis was the turning point in the evolution of the Chinese view from minimalism to unprecedented activism in multilateral diplomacy.'[27]

After the Tiananmen crackdown and the collapse of communism in Eastern Europe and the Soviet Union, China was isolated internationally. Under a siege mentality, Deng advised that China should keep a low profile internationally, while concentrating on economic reform at home. The Jiang government acted cautiously to break the US-led Western sanctions on China. After the relaxation of the Tiananmen sanctions, in early 1995 Jiang turned his attention to Taiwan by promulgating an eight-point initiative on peaceful reunification. Jiang realized the importance of championing the nationalist cause, not least for the sake of propping up the CCP's legitimacy. But the use of coercive diplomacy against Taiwan in the name of national unification backfired. Likewise, nationalism proved to be a double-edged sword during the anti-Japanese demonstrations over the Diaoyu Islands in 1996. The Jiang government had to reconcile the tension between appealing to the nationalist cause and containing the growth of popular nationalism.

After the 1995–6 events, China more proactively embraced multi-lateralism to improve its international status and influence. The cultivation of China's identity as a responsible great power would also boost Jiang's political authority at home.

Notes

1 Lu Ning, 'The Central Leadership, Supraministry Coordinating Bodies, State Council Ministries, and Party Departments', in David M. Lampton (ed.), *The Making of Chinese Foreign and Security Policy in the Era of Reform* (Stanford: Stanford University Press, 2001), 40–1.
2 See Joseph Fewsmith, *China since Tiananmen: From Deng Xiaoping to Hu Jintao*, 2nd edition (Cambridge: Cambridge University Press, 2008), 21–47.
3 *Selected Works of Deng Xiaoping,* vol. iii, 305–11.
4 See John W. Garver, 'The Chinese Communist Party and the Collapse of Soviet Communism', *CQ* 133 (March 1993): 1–26.
5 Qian Qichen, *Ten Episodes in China's Diplomacy* (New York: HarperCollins Publishers, 2005), 31.
6 David M. Lampton, *Same Bed, Different Dreams: Managing U.S.–China Relations, 1989–2000* (Berkeley: University of California Press, 2001), 17–18, 21–30.
7 Qian, op. cit., 135.
8 Ibid., 149–50, 153–5.
9 Ibid., 144–9.
10 Lampton, op. cit., 33–4.
11 See Rosemary Foot, *Rights beyond Borders: The Global Community and the Struggle over Human Rights in China* (Oxford: Oxford University Press, 2000), 137–57.
12 Lampton, op. cit., 39–45.
13 Fewsmith, op. cit., 62–3, 72.
14 Foot, op. cit., 158–65.
15 Lampton, op. cit., 382.
16 H. Lyman Miller and Liu Xiaohong, 'The Foreign Policy Outlook of China's "Third Generation" Elite', in Lampton (ed.), op. cit., 123–50.; Willy Wo-lap Lam, *The Era of Jiang Zemin* (Singapore: Prentice Hall, 1999), 360–1.
17 Michael D. Swaine, 'Chinese Decision-Making Regarding Taiwan, 1979–2000', in Lampton (ed.), op. cit., 313–14.
18 Qian, op. cit., 244.
19 See Erica Strecker Downs and Philip C. Saunders, 'Legitimacy and the Limits of Nationalism: China and the Diaoyu Islands', *IS* 23: 3 (Winter 1998/99): 114–46; Peter Hays Gries, *China's New Nationalism: Pride, Politics, and Diplomacy* (Berkeley: University of California Press, 2004), 121–5.

20 See Gries, op. cit., 125–8.
21 Yong Deng, *China's Struggle for Status: The Realignment of International Relations* (Cambridge: Cambridge University Press, 2008), 104–10.
22 Robert Sutter, 'China's Regional Strategy and Why It May Not be Good for America', in David Shambaugh (ed.), *Power Shift: China and Asia's New Dynamics* (Berkeley: University of California Press, 2005), 290.
23 On this theme, see Rosemary Foot, 'Chinese Power and the Idea of a Responsible State', *The China Journal* 45 (January 2001): 1–19.
24 See James Mann, *About Face: A History of America's Curious Relationship with China, from Nixon to Clinton* (New York: Alfred A. Knopf, 1999), 353–68.
25 See Gries, op. cit., 98–108, 128–33.
26 Samuel S. Kim, 'China and the United Nations', in Michael Oksenberg and Elizabeth Economy (eds), *China Joins the World: Progress and Prospects* (New York: Council on Foreign Relations Press, 1999), 80.
27 Michael Yahuda, *The International Politics of the Asia-Pacific*, 2nd edition (London: RoutledgeCurzon, 2004), 298; Robert G. Sutter, *Chinese Foreign Relations: Power and Policy since the Cold War*, 2nd edition (Lanham: Rowman & Littlefield, 2010), 233.

10 The rise of China in the twenty-first century

This chapter outlines the rise, or re-emergence, of China as a dominant force in Asia in the first decade of the twenty-first century. Indeed, China became not only a regional great power but also a candidate super-power. In 1998 China successfully staged arguably the most majestic and expensive Olympic Games in history. When the sixtieth anniversary of the founding of the People's Republic was celebrated the following year, China was fundamentally different from what it had been in 1949: a stronger, richer, and more confident nation.

Economic globalization

In December 2001, China joined the WTO after 15 years of negotiations, including the protracted talks on China's restoration of its status in the GATT. To bring the negotiations to a successful conclusion, in 1999 the Chinese government had made substantial concessions to America regarding tariff reduction, agricultural subsidies, protection of intellectual property rights, and the opening of the banking sector. In the age of growing economic globalization, the Chinese leaders realized that to sustain its economic growth, China needed to forge even closer links with the global economy. The augmentation of China's 'comprehensive national power' was essential to domestic stability and regime survival. Through its WTO membership, China expected to play a greater role in shaping the rules and norms of the global trading regime. As far as Sino-American relations were concerned, Beijing hoped to restrain Washington's unilateralism and hegemony in the webs of deepening economic interdependence.[1]

After WTO accession, China's economy continued to bloom. In 2004 China overtook Japan as the world's third largest trading economy, after the European Union (EU) and the United States. Between 2004 and 2007, China doubled the size of its exports, surpassing

America as the world's largest exporter. China enjoyed a trade surplus of US$34 billion in 2004, and of US$102 billion the next year. It had the world's largest foreign exchange reserves, and was one of the largest destinations of foreign direct investment. In the three decades since economic reform, China's gross domestic product increased from 1 to over 5 per cent of the world total. In 2007 it contributed to more than 10 per cent of the growth in the world economy.[2] The global financial crisis of 2007–8 and the ensuing economic downturn adversely affected China's exports and resulted in the unemployment of millions of rural–urban migrants. Yet China did not suffer from a 'credit crunch', and generally avoided a technical recession. In 2009 China still enjoyed an impressive growth rate of 8 per cent.[3] Together with the world's largest population, a permanent seat in the UN Security Council, a nuclear arsenal, and an ambitious space programme, the People's Republic possessed the attributes of a global superpower.

New leaders and new ideas

Just as Jiang Zemin had been hand-picked as the nucleus of the 'third generation', the late Deng Xiaoping, too, engineered the transition to power to Hu Jintao as the 'fourth generation' leadership. A former Party chief in Gansu, Guizhou, and Tibet, Hu became General Secretary of the CCP in 2002, and was concurrently State President from 2003 and Chairman of the Central Military Commission from 2004. As the paramount leader, Hu was served by Premier Wen Jiabao and other fourth generation leaders who shared similar characteristics: 'technocratic' backgrounds (i.e. engineering, industry, and economics by training), the best-educated cohort in CCP history, and the experiences of the Cultural Revolution.[4] Although commanding Party, state, and military power, Hu attached importance to consensus-building in policy-making. In the age of globalization, China's interests and involvement in the world economy, multilateral security institutions, and transnational issues increased substantially. So did the number of actors involved in the shaping of Chinese foreign policy, for example economic bureaucracies, non-governmental think-tanks, coastal provinces, and even 'public opinion'. Of course, Hu and Wen retained ultimate control over China's foreign and domestic policy, but the diversification of the decision-making process was a prominent trend.

Domestically, the Hu–Wen team regarded economic development and social stability as policy priorities. In foreign affairs, one of the main challenges was the international community's perceptions of, and responses to, the 'rise' of China as an economic and military power.

Thus, Hu, Wen, and their think-tanks formulated a number of new concepts to guide China's foreign policy. In November 2003, Zheng Bijian coined the term 'peaceful rise' (*heping jueqi*) to argue that China's ascendance would not be a threat to the world order, unlike the challenges posed by Germany, Japan, and the Soviet Union in the past. (In 2005 Zheng elaborated on this theme in an article titled 'China's "Peaceful Rise" to Great-Power Status', published in the US journal *Foreign Affairs*.) An influential Party theoretician, Zheng was a trusted adviser to Hu, who had headed the CCP Party School where Zheng worked in the late 1990s. Later, Wen and Hu both used the term 'peaceful rise' in their public speeches. But in view of the fact that the word *jueqi* ('rising abruptly') might be linked with the 'decline' or 'fall' of other powers by the Westerners, the Hu–Wen team was inclined to use 'peaceful development' (*heping fazhan*). In April 2004 President Hu, addressing the Boao Forum on Asia, spoke of the peaceful development path that China had been taking, a path that was economic-oriented, non-hegemonistic, and beneficial to the whole world.[5]

Underpinning the concept of 'peaceful rise/development' was the notion of building a 'harmonious world' (*hexie shijie*). The latter in turn derived from the vision of building a 'socialist harmonious society', articulated by Hu, that emphasized fairness, justice, trustworthiness, and the rule of law.[6] (There was a gap between Hu's vision and the reality of CCP's authoritarian rule, though.) At the sixtieth anniversary summit of the UN in September 2005, Hu enunciated the concept of building a 'harmonious world'. All countries should abandon the Cold War mentality, and embrace multilateralism and a 'new security concept featuring trust, mutual benefit, equality and cooperation'. Economic cooperation should be 'mutually beneficial to all parties', and the world trading system 'open, fair, and non-discriminatory'. All countries should strive to 'make international relations more democratic'. Lastly, Hu envisioned reforming the UN 'in a rational way when necessary'. At the Seventeenth Party Congress in 2007, Hu called for the building of a 'harmonious world' of 'lasting peace and common prosperity'.[7]

Hu's vision of a 'harmonious world' was grounded in both Chinese traditional philosophy and contemporary challenges. In line with Confucianism emphasizing orderly peace, benevolence, and harmony, Hu's was a world that allowed for diversity, interdependence, mutual benefits, and peaceful resolution of conflicts. Moreover, Hu built on the ideas of his predecessors, such as the 'new security concept' advocated by Jiang in 1997 and the Five Principles of Peaceful Coexistence promulgated by Zhou Enlai in the mid-1950s. By promoting the notion of a world of 'lasting peace and common prosperity', Hu hoped to counter the 'China threat' theories propagated by neo-conservatives in the United States and elsewhere. But the 'harmonious world' idea was not merely peace rhetoric to reassure the world or pragmatic response to US unilateralism under the Bush administration. Rather, Hu and his advisors held the conviction that 'democratizing' existing international institutions and norms would change the world for the better. It demonstrated the growing confidence on the part of the fourth generation leadership that China could and should play a more active role in building a fairer world. To the new leaders, China's identity was as a responsible great power, which aimed to reform but not displace the US-dominated global order.[8]

China's all-directional diplomacy

The Sino-American relationship was the centrepiece of China's diplomacy. By the turn of the century, the two economies had become inter-dependent, with China relying on the American market for its cheap consumer goods while America depended on the Chinese purchases of US government bonds. But on the other hand, mutual suspicions coloured Sino-American interactions. When George W. Bush entered the White House in 2001, Sino-American relations got off to a rocky start. Initially viewing China as a 'strategic competitor' rather than a 'strategic partner', the Bush administration reversed Clinton's 'three nos' policy regarding Taiwan by reinvigorating US commitment to Taipei such as the approval of expensive weapons sales including submarines.[9] Then came the American spy plane collision. On 1 April, a Chinese F-8 fighter jet collided with an American EP-3 surveillance aircraft over the South China Sea, which resulted in the killing of the Chinese pilot and the EP-3's emergency landing on China's Hainan Island. It triggered a diplomatic row between the two sides; Beijing demanded a formal apology from Washington and detained the American crew for 11 days. For the Chinese government and nationalists, the main issue was China's 'lost face' – the sense of 'victimization' at the hands of 'Western imperialism' – which could only be redeemed by American apologies. Eventually, after intense negotiations over the wording, the Americans sent a letter to the Chinese government, stating that they were 'very sorry' for the killing of the Chinese pilot and for the entry of the American plane into China's airspace and its landing on Hainan without prior permission.[10]

The terrorist attacks on New York and Washington on 11 September completely changed the dynamic of Sino-American relations. Pre-occupied with the 'war on terror' in Afghanistan, Iraq, and elsewhere, and hoping for China's support, the Bush administration took steps to repair Sino-American relations. For its part, China seized the opportunity to promote its international image as a responsible, cooperative great power. It also sought Washington's support for its own 'anti-terror' war against Uighur separatism in Xinjiang, thereby countering international criticism of human rights violations there. Thus, China shared intelligence with Washington, joined the US efforts against money laundering by suspected terrorists, and supported the US Container Security Initiative to screen cargoes destined for America. While harbouring serious reservations about a US invasion of Iraq in 2003, Beijing carefully avoided direct confrontation with Washington and instead let Russia and France take the lead in opposing US policy at the UN.

Sino-American divergences over Taiwan narrowed in the midst of anti-terror cooperation. On the other hand, the gap between Washington and Taipei increasingly widened as a result of the pro-independence initiatives taken by the Democratic Progressive Party leader, Chen Shui-bian, who was elected Taiwan's president in 2000. In October 2002, Jiang Zemin, during his informal summit with President G. W. Bush at the latter's ranch in Crawford, Texas, sought to strengthen Sino-American cooperation over Taiwan. Jiang proposed that China move an unspecified number of mobile missiles from its south-eastern coast opposite Taiwan if America agreed to reduce, and eventually end, arms sales to Taiwan. Although the US administration was unresponsive to Jiang's proposal, Bush nonetheless promised to develop a 'constructive, cooperative, and candid' relationship with China. In view of Chen Shui-bian's ambitious pursuit of his hidden agenda of Taiwan's independence through proposed referenda on a number of issues such as membership of the World Health Organization, the Bush administration came to regard Taipei as an embarrassment and an obstacle to improved Sino-American relations. In December 2003, Bush confided to Premier Wen Jiabao that Washington would 'oppose any unilateral decision by either China or Taiwan to change the status quo', drawing attention to the 'comments and actions made by the leader of Taiwan'.[11]

After re-election in 2004, Chen stepped up his independence rhetoric and initiatives. But the Chinese leaders had learnt the lessons of the 1995–6 Taiwan Strait Crisis and de-emphasized the use of coercive diplomacy against Taiwan (although they still refused to renounce the use of force against the island and passed a tough anti-secession law in March 2005). Instead, China relied on 'strategic dialogues' with the United States, in the hope that Washington and Beijing would develop a better understanding of each other's views and interests including Taiwan. In 2006 China and America established the Strategic Economic Dialogue between the US Secretary of the Treasury and the Chinese Vice-Premier, which met biannually to discuss economic issues, and the Senior Dialogue, conducted by the US Deputy Secretary of State, which focused on Sino-American political relations. With the election of Guomindang Chairman Ma Ying-jeou as President in March 2008, China–Taiwan relations gradually improved. In November that year, Taiwan for the first time agreed to China's requests for direct shipping and air services. As a result of growing cross-Strait interactions, Sino-American relations also stabilized.

China expanded its 'strategic partnership' with Russia, first formed in 1996. In July 2001, China and Russia signed the Treaty of Good-Neighbourliness and Friendly Cooperation, which included 25 articles covering a wide range of issues such as security cooperation, economic contacts, and border issues. Although not directed towards any third party, the treaty was partly a response to American unilateralism under the new Bush administration. Nevertheless, neither China nor Russia desired to return to the Cold War-style alliance relationship of the 1950s. Indeed, both countries still saw their respective relationship with America as more important than their partnership. Beijing and Moscow, moreover, intensified security cooperation in Central Asia. In July 2001 the Shanghai Cooperation Organization (SCO) was founded – the expansion and institutionalization of the original 'Shanghai Five' security regime, established in 1996, with the addition of Uzbekistan. China's leading role was crystal clear: the SCO's secretariat was located in and funded by Beijing. The SCO leaders held annual summits. In October 2002, the first military training exercise between China and Kyrgyzstan was held. In August 2003, a much larger exercise involving China, Russia, Kazakhstan, Kyrgyzstan, and Tajikistan was conducted.[12]

To foster a peaceful peripheral environment for its economic development, China became more proactive in engaging its Asian neighbours and regional multilateral institutions. China deepened its involvement in the ASEAN and the ASEAN Regional Forum (ARF). During the ARF meeting in July 2002, the Chinese delegation for the first time submitted a formal position paper enunciating the 'new security concept'. In November, China and ASEAN signed the Declaration on the Conduct of Parties in the South China Sea, whereby they agreed to take no unilateral and military steps that would increase the potential for conflict in the disputed islands. At the October 2003 summit, China and the ten ASEAN states agreed to establish the Strategic Partnership for Peace and Prosperity, which was 'non-aligned, non-military, and non-exclusive' in nature. Its main objectives were to promote strategic dialogues, enhance mutual understanding, and strengthen cooperation over non-traditional security issues. Simultaneously, China signed up to the ASEAN Treaty of Amity and Cooperation, committing itself to refraining from the use of force for settling disputes.[13]

In November 2002, a formal agreement was signed on establishing a China–ASEAN free-trade zone by 2010. As a first step, in 2004 China unilaterally opened its markets to over 600 products from the bordering ASEAN states, thus demonstrating that its economic growth represented an opportunity rather than a threat to its neighbours. During the Severe Acute Respiratory Syndrome (SARS) Crisis in 2003, Premier Wen Jiaobao, when visiting Bangkok, admitted the initially inadequate Chinese response and pledged full cooperation with other Asian countries over combating the transnational disease outbreak. Later in June, China sponsored an ASEAN Plus Three meeting focusing on anti-SARS cooperation. Besides, China supported the ASEAN's idea of the East Asian Summit, with its inaugural meeting being held in Kuala Lumpur in December 2005. Although Beijing had preferred an all-East Asian community to a diverse membership of 16 countries including India, Australia, and New Zealand, it valued the East Asian Summit as another forum for tackling transnational issues such as trade, energy, and environment.[14]

China played a more active mediating role in the Korean nuclear crisis. In October 2002, North Korea resumed its weapons-grade uranium enrichment programme in violation of the 1994 Agreed Framework. In August 2003, China hosted the Six-Party Talks between America, the two Koreas, Japan, Russia, and China. Between 2004 and 2007, China shuttled among the five capitals, keeping Washington engaged and exerting pressure on Pyongyang. In September 2005, China hammered out a Six-Party Agreement, according to which the signatories pledged to commit to a nuclear-free Korean peninsula, and America and Japan agreed to provide energy aid and gradually normalize relations with North Korea. While averting the economic collapse of North Korea was a key objective, China's multilateral diplomacy was also motivated by the desire for being recognized as a responsible great power in resolving international disputes.[15]

Yet in October 2006, North Korea, disregarding China's calls for restraint, conducted its first nuclear/missile test. Beijing went along with the UN resolution condemning the nuclear test and imposing sanctions on North Korea. Although China paid only lip service to the implementation of UN sanctions (particularly concerning the inspection of North Korean cargo ships), it successfully persuaded North Korea to return to the Six-Party Talks in December. In February 2007, North Korea agreed to dismantle its nuclear facility in Yongbyon and permit international verification. But Pyongyang dragged its feet later, conducting its second nuclear test in May 2009. As the only key ally and the main trading partner of North Korea, nonetheless, China remained the only power that could wield influence over the unpredictable and paranoid Communist regime.

China faced more challenges in its dealings with Japan, which were characterized by 'cold politics and hot economics'.[16] On the one hand, the history textbook issue, repeated visits by Japanese Prime Minister Koizumi to the Yasukuni Shrine, and the dispute over the Diaoyu Islands hampered political relations. On the other hand, China and Japan became economically interdependent in terms of trading and investment. In the mid-2000s, Sino-Japanese relations were strained due to a mix of international and domestic factors: the rise of China and the resurgence of Japan's assertiveness after decades of economic stagnation, intensified competition over gas and oil resources in the East China Sea, and contending popular nationalisms in the age of the Internet. The Diaoyu Islands became the site of territorial and resource dispute.

In April 2005, violent and large-scale anti-Japanese demonstrations erupted in Beijing and other Chinese cities. The demonstrators were provoked by the Japanese occupation of the lighthouse on Uotsuri Island in February, Tokyo's authorization of new history textbooks that glossed over Japan's war responsibilities in April, and Japan's bid for a permanent UN Security Council seat. Mobilized through the Internet and mobile phones, nationalistic Chinese youth took to the streets in their thousands, attacking Japanese diplomatic properties and businesses. Nevertheless, the Chinese government was anxious to contain the growth of Chinese mass nationalism, lest Sino-Japanese economic relations would be jeopardized. It wanted to ensure that the Chinese 'online nationalists', frustrated with the domestic social and political situation, would not turn against their own government in the name of anti-Japanese agitation – thus, the ban on 'unauthorized' demonstrations and activities and the promotion of 'patriotic education'. After the 2005 events, China and Japan sought to reduce political tension so that they could concentrate on economic interactions. By mid-2008, after rounds of negotiations, they agreed to the joint development of maritime resources in the East China Sea, while shelving the contentious sovereignty issue.[17]

Beyond Asia, China strengthened its ties with the European Union (EU), which by 2005 included 25 European states. During the 2000s, China–EU trade and European investment in China expanded substantially. By 2004, for the first time, the EU became China's largest trading partner, accounting for 19 per cent of its total trade. China was the second largest trading partner of the EU.[18] China and the EU, moreover, conducted a number of dialogues on economic issues, ranging from industrial policy and regulation to space science and energy technology.

China–EU politico-strategic cooperation entered a mature stage. In 2003 China and the EU strove to build a 'strategic partnership'. In September the European Commission adopted a policy paper entitled 'A Maturing Partnership: Shared Interests and Challenges in EU–China Relations', and the next month China published its first ever policy paper on the EU. In view of the economic rise of China, the EU hoped to deepen China's involvement in 'global governance'. For its part, China had gained a new appreciation of the EU as an independent political and economic force as a result of the launch of the euro, the formation of a Rapid Reaction Force, and the anti-war stance on Iraq taken by France, Germany, and others. The China–EU Strategic Partnership aimed to promote multilateral cooperation and dialogues over not only traditional security issues but also new global challenges such as climate change, energy security, and human trafficking.[19] In December 2005, the first China–EU Strategic Dialogue at Vice-Foreign Minister Level was held in London, covering China–EU relations, North Korea, and energy security.

In 2008, however, China's relations with a number of European countries were strained over Tibet and human rights generally. As a result of Beijing's suppression of Tibetan demonstrations in March, pro-Tibetan and human rights activists protested against the Olympic torch relay in Paris and London, and some European leaders talked of boycotting the opening ceremony of the Olympic Games in Beijing later in the summer. On the other hand, the Chinese leaders and young Chinese nationalists felt that the Western media had been biased in its coverage of the Tibetan demonstrations (which allegedly ignored the Tibetans' violence against the Han Chinese) and that the protests against the Olympic torch relay were deliberate attempts to disrupt China's fulfilment of its 'hundred-year dream' – or to 'humiliate' China in the modern age.[20] In the end, though, the Beijing Olympics was a huge success, and no Western leader dared to boycott it. In short, despite its economic performance, China's human rights record continued to attract international attention and criticism from time to time.

China gave prominence to relations with African countries. Politically, Beijing was alert to Taiwan's attempts to buy recognition and influence in Africa through 'money diplomacy'. Since the late 1990s, China attached particular importance to energy resources in Africa, not least to reduce its dependence on the Middle East and Russia for the supply of oil and gas. As the world's largest consumer of oil, China struck oil deals with Nigeria, Sudan, and Angola. In addition, Chinese companies exported textiles and manufactured goods to a number of African countries, and invested heavily in the continent.

China, meanwhile, increased its political role in African affairs. In October 2000 the first China–Africa Cooperation Forum, attended by the leaders of 45 African countries, was held in Beijing, discussing economic and political cooperation. At the gathering, China pledged to write off US$1.2 billion in African debt and to increase foreign aid to Africa. China also contributed to UN peacekeeping missions in Africa, including the Democratic Republic of Congo, Liberia, and Sudan. In the case of Sudan, an important oil supplier, although China had been reluctant to condemn alleged war crimes in Darfur in 2004, it did make efforts to persuade Khartoum to engage with the UN and outside powers in resolving the Darfur crisis.[21]

China also made diplomatic inroads into the Middle East and Latin America, out of consideration for energy security. China imported large amounts of Iranian oil and gas, and invested in Iranian energy infrastructure. Likewise, China's energy diplomacy targeted a number of Latin American countries, such as Brazil, Venezuela, Bolivia, and Colombia.

A prominent feature of China's diplomacy in the twenty-first century was its increasing reliance on 'soft power' – the use of Chinese culture and ideas to influence foreign governments and peoples. Thus, China established 'Confucian Institutes' abroad for the study of Chinese language and culture, attracted foreign students and tourists to the mainland, staged international sporting events such as the 2008 Olympic Games, and facilitated the 'globalization' of Chinese products such as food, art, and cheap consumer goods. Chinese diplomats overseas also became more cosmopolitan in outlook and sophisticated in reaching out to the host society. Although China's political values and autocratic system still lacked global appeal, as compared with Western liberalism and democracies, there is no denying that the use of its 'soft power' in other aspects was successful.[22]

China: threat or peaceful rise?

In the first decade of the millennium, then, China actively pursued strategic partnerships, multilateral diplomacy, and economic globalization. Did China's conciliatory approach aim to hide its great-power aspirations and expansion? Did China have a grand strategy to challenge the status quo and ultimately replace the United States as the predominant power in the world?

Joshua Kurlantzick has examined how China exploited its growing 'soft power' for foreign and domestic policy objectives. By promoting the visions of a 'harmonious world' and China's 'peaceful rise/development', Beijing aimed to counter the 'China threat' theories and prevent the global containment of China. China's diplomatic activities in Africa were intended to secure oil and other resources to power its ever-growing economy and military machinery. Above all, China's 'charm offensive' was meant to woo friends and hide its great-power ambitions.[23]

Some International Relations and China scholars argue that since the turn of the century a 'power transition' between the United States and China has been taking place. According to the 'power transition' theory, the rising China, dissatisfied with the status quo, was (and is) seeking to replace the incumbent superpower, the United States, as the hegemonic power in the world, a challenge that, as the history of rising anti-status quo powers has shown, would result in war.[24] In developing strategic partnerships with other powers, and engaging with multilateral regional security institutions, so the theory goes, China aimed primarily to balance US power and influence on its periphery.

Other scholars contend that instead of balancing America through anti-hegemonic coalitions, China has been pursuing a 'soft-bandwagoning' strategy by accommodating the US primacy in the world. By the early 2000s, China came to realize that a multipolar world was unlikely to emerge in the foreseeable future and that the American presence in Asia was long-standing and could not be easily replaced. Instead, China recognized America's essential stabilizing roles in the region, notably on the resurgence of Japanese power. According to Rosemary Foot, besides accommodating the United States, China simultaneously pursued a 'hedging strategy' or an 'insurance policy' by increasing its military power and diplomatic influence.[25] The aim was to prepare China for every contingency in the uncertain international environment, for example deterring, or, failing that, countering, Taiwan's declaration of independence and America's support for the island.

In essence, China had neither the capability nor the intention of directly challenging America's military and political predominance in Asia. Notwithstanding double-digit increases in its defence budget and the modernization of its military force, China was anxious to avert a Cold War-style arms race with America. With no aircraft carriers or long-range bombers, China lacked capabilities to project power on a global scale. In terms of overall military strength and nuclear technology, there remained a huge gap between China and the United States. The focus of China's military modernization and expansion was Taiwan. Preoccupied with mounting internal problems such as social inequalities and ethnic and rural unrest, and aware of the declining legitimacy of the Communist ideology, the Chinese leaders placed a premium on domestic economic development and stable Sino-American relations.[26] After all, China was, as Susan Shirk put it, a 'fragile superpower'. If China were a threat, it was its 'internal fragility' that might present 'the greatest danger' to the world in the event that the economy slowed down and the Communist regime pursued aggressive foreign policy to divert domestic discontent.[27]

Notes

1 Thomas G. Moore, 'Chinese Foreign Policy in the Age of Globalization', in Yong Deng and Fei-Ling Wang (eds), *China Rising: Power and Motivation in Chinese Foreign Policy* (Lanham: Rowman & Littlefield, 2005), 121–58.

2 Robert G. Sutter, *Chinese Foreign Relations: Power and Policy since the Cold War*, 2nd edition (Lanham: Rowman & Littlefield, 2010), 70–1; Li Lanqing, translated by Ling Yuan and Zhang Siying, *Breaking Through: The Birth of China's Opening-up Policy* (New York: Oxford University Press, 2009), 425–6.

3 Linda Yueh, 'China and the Global Financial Crisis: Responses and Outlook', *China Review* 50 (Summer 2010): 23–5.

4 David Shambaugh, *China's Communist Party: Atrophy and Adaptation* (Washington, D.C.: Woodrow Wilson Center Press, 2008), 152–7.

5 David M. Lampton, *The Three Faces of Chinese Power: Might, Money, and Minds* (Berkeley: University of California Press, 2008), 33–4.

6 Shambaugh, op. cit., 115–16.

7 Jean-Marc F. Blanchard and Sujian Guo, 'Introduction: "Harmonious World" and China's New Foreign Policy', in Jean-Marc F. Blanchard and Sujian Guo (eds), *'Harmonious World' and China's New Foreign Policy* (Lanham: Rowman & Littefield, 2008), 2–3.

8 Ibid., 4–6; Rosemary Foot, 'Chinese Strategies in a US-Hegemonic Global Order: Accommodating and Hedging', *International Affairs* 82: 1 (January 2006): 90–3.

9 See Nancy Bernkopf Tucker, *Strait Talk: United States–Taiwan Relations and the Crisis with China* (Cambridge, Mass.: Harvard University Press, 2009), 251–72.

10 Peter Hays Gries, *China's New Nationalism: Pride, Politics, and Diplomacy* (Berkeley: University of California Press, 2004), 86–90, 108–13.

11 Quoted in Tucker, op. cit., 268.

12 Yu Bin, 'China and Russia: Normalizing Their Strategic Partnership', in David Shambaugh (ed.), *Power Shift: China and Asia's New Dynamics* (Berkeley: University of California Press, 2005), 234–41.

13 Bates Gill, 'China's Evolving Regional Security Strategy', in ibid., 254–7.

14 Yong Deng, *China's Struggle for Status: The Realignment of International Relations* (Cambridge: Cambridge University Press, 2008), 225–7.

15 Ibid., 205–16.

16 On this theme, see Min Gyo Koo, 'The Senkaku/Diaoyu Dispute and Sino-Japanese Political-Economic Relations: Cold Politics and Hot Economics?', *The Pacific Review* 22: 2 (May 2009): 205–32.

17 Ibid., 225–7.
18 Robert Ash, 'Europe's Commercial Relations with China', in David Shambaugh, Eberhard Sandschneider, and Zhou Hong (eds), *China–Europe Relations: Perceptions, Policies and Prospects* (London: Routledge, 2008), 213.
19 Feng Zhongping, 'Promoting the Deeper Development of China–EU Relations', in David Kerr and Liu Fei (eds), *The International Politics of EU–China Relations* (Oxford: Oxford University Press, 2007), 268–71.
20 William A. Callahan, *China: The Pessoptimist Nation* (Oxford: Oxford University Press, 2010), 9–10.
21 Sutter, op. cit., 310–23.
22 Lampton, op. cit., 142–4, 152–63.
23 Joshua Kurlantzick, *Charm Offensive: How China's Soft Power is Transforming the World* (New Haven: Yale University Press, 2007), 37–42.
24 For different views on the Sino-American 'power transition', see Robert S. Ross and Zhu Feng (eds), *China's Ascent: Power, Security, and the Future of International Politics* (Ithaca: Cornell University Press, 2008).
25 Foot, op. cit., 88.
26 Zhu Feng, 'China's Rise Will Be Peaceful: How Unipolarity Matters', in Ross and Zhu (eds), op. cit., 34–54.
27 Susan L. Shirk, *China: Fragile Superpower* (New York: Oxford University Press, 2007), 255.

Conclusion

Throughout history China has been actively engaging with the outside world through trade, migration, and cultural transfer – as well as warfare. During the Republican period, China 'witnessed a qualitatively unprecedented trend towards openness' in terms of governance, borders, markets, and ideas.[1] Communist China was not isolationist either. During the 1950s, Mao's China was an integral part of the Soviet socialist world. In the early 1970s, after Sino-American rapprochement, China joined the international community. But if Mao normalized relations with America mainly for strategic reasons (countering the Soviet threat), in the 1980s Deng Xiaoping embraced the US-led global order in order to secure American capital and technology for China's modernization. In the post-Deng era, Jiang Zemin and Hu Jintao further enmeshed China within the global economy and the webs of relationships with the United States. By 2009, when it celebrated its sixtieth anniversary, the PRC was part and parcel of the globalized world.

After the 'century of humiliation', China was in constant search of a new national identity on the world stage. Successive CCP leaders were determined to rid China of the legacies of imperialism, inequalities, and injustices. In 1949 Mao made his 'leaning to one side' speech, proclaiming that New China was a close ally of the Soviet Union. As an underdeveloped nation, however, China also possessed a 'Third World identity'. With similar experiences of foreign imperialism, China identified with the world's oppressed peoples and their fight for national independence. In the mid-1950s, Zhou Enlai enunciated the Five Principles of Peaceful Coexistence, calling for all countries, regardless of size and political system, to respect national sovereignty and territorial integrity, non-aggression, non-interference in internal affairs, and mutual benefit. These principles were not empty peace rhetoric but enduring ideals that lay at the heart of China's search for a new identity after 1949.

Until the late 1950s, China's identities as a Communist state and a Third World nation coexisted quite easily. As long as the Soviet Union held high the banner of anti-imperialism and supported China's economic and military development, Mao was willing to subordinate China's national interest to proletarian internationalism. But with the intensification of the Sino-Soviet split, Mao could no longer tolerate 'Soviet big power chauvinism' and China's subordinate status. After breaking with the Soviet revisionists, in the mid-1960s, China positioned itself within the 'intermediate zone' of Asian–African–Latin American nations. Mao saw China as the leader of the wars of national liberation in the Third World, and rendered massive assistance to North Vietnam in its anti-colonial struggle against the United States.

With the outbreak of the Cultural Revolution in 1966, China took on the two superpowers and seemingly 30 other countries. But for all his revolutionary rhetoric, Mao indeed did not intend to make enemies of the entire world. Following a series of attacks on foreign embassies including the sacking of the British Chargé Office in Beijing in the summer of 1967, Mao and Zhou were anxious to restore some degree of normality to China's diplomacy and foreign relations. The ideological Mao was pragmatic enough to make realistic calculations of China's national interest. This was especially so after 1969, when the escalating Sino-Soviet Border War raised the spectre of a nuclear attack on China. Confronted with the intensified Soviet threat, together with the fading status of his 'continuous revolution', Mao decided to normalize relations with the United States.

After the Nixon visit in 1972, China became, in Kissinger's words, America's 'tacit ally'. But with the eclipse of an imminent Soviet threat, Mao harboured second thoughts on the implication of Sino-American normalization for China's relations with the Third World. He struggled between strategic alignment with the American imperialists and China's identity as a champion of the oppressed nations. In 1974 Mao put forward the Theory of Three Worlds, opposing both Soviet and American hegemonies and identifying China with the underdeveloped nations in Asia, Africa, and Latin America. But with the renewal of the Soviet threat in the late 1970s, Deng Xiaoping, who succeeded the late Mao, decided to expedite Sino-American diplomatic normalization. Intended to launch a massive programme of economic reform and opening-up, Deng needed American capital and technology. He saw China's future as being tied to the US-led global economy.

Since 1979 Sino-American ties have strengthened at all levels. Nonetheless, due to the Reagan administration's continued arms sales to the island, the Taiwan issue re-emerged as an irritant in Sino-American relations. In 1982 Deng proclaimed an 'independent foreign policy', setting national unification with Taiwan, Hong Kong, and Macao as one of

China's three main tasks in the decade. At a time when Communist ideology was losing its legitimacy in the age of unprecedented economic reform, appeals to nationalism became more important than ever. However, in 1989 the Tiananmen student demonstrations plunged the CCP into a profound legitimacy crisis.

After the Tiananmen crackdown and the collapse of communism in Eastern Europe and the Soviet Union, China redefined its identity and role on the world stage. Following Deng's advice, China kept a low profile in foreign affairs. To prop up the declining legitimacy of the CCP, Jiang Zemin appealed to Chinese nationalism: he made his eight-point initiative on peaceful reunification with Taiwan. But when Taipei refused to reciprocate, in 1995–6 Jiang resorted to coercive diplomacy in the Taiwan Strait, triggering a crisis with the United States. After the confrontation over Taiwan, Jiang and Clinton sought to re-establish a consensus on Sino-American cooperation through summitry. The summit meetings in 1997 and 1998 marked a turning point in Sino-American relations and in China's diplomacy generally. In the latter half of the 1990s, China embraced more actively multilateralism and economic globalization. Concerned about China's international status and his personal legacy, Jiang endeavoured to promote China's identity as a responsible state in the world.

Into the twenty-first century, China has deepened its engagement with global institutions and norms. Hu Jintao's government has been promoting the notion of China's 'peaceful rise/development' and the building of a 'harmonious world'. The main challenge for the international community is whether China really adheres to its proclaimed 'peaceful and responsible power' identity or it merely hides its great-power aspirations behind a charm offensive. With the further growth of its economic and military power in the future, China may become more aggressive and intolerant, seeking to challenge the status quo and US supremacy by war. Or conversely, China has been so enmeshed in the global economic and political order that any aggressive challenge to the status quo will put its own economy and social stability in jeopardy.

This chapter does not aim to make predictions of China's future development. But hopefully readers can draw their own conclusions after reviewing China's international history since 1945 – how China defined its identity and engaged with the wider world after the 'century of humiliation'.

Note

1 On this argument, see Frank Dikötter, *The Age of Openness: China before Mao* (Hong Kong: Hong Kong University Press, 2008).

Further Reading

Barnouin, B. and Yu, C., *Chinese Foreign Policy During the Cultural Revolution*, London: Kegan Paul International, 1998.

Bernstein, T.P. and Li, H.–Y., eds, *China Learns from the Soviet Union, 1949– Present*, Lanham: Rowman & Littlefield, 2010.

Brown, J. and Pickowicz, P.G., eds, *Dilemmas of Victory: The Early Years of the People's Republic of China*, Cambridge, Mass.: Harvard University Press, 2007.

Callahan, W.A., *China: The Pessoptimist Nation*, Oxford: Oxford University Press, 2010.

Chen, J., *China's Road to the Korean War: The Making of the Sino-American Confrontation*, New York: Columbia University Press, 1994.

Chen, J., *Mao's China and the Cold War*, Chapel Hill: The University of North Carolina Press, 2001.

Dittmer, L., *Sino-Soviet Normalization and Its International Implications 1945– 1990*, Seattle: University of Washington Press, 1992.

Foot, R., *Rights beyond Borders: The Global Community and the Struggle over Human Rights in China*, Oxford: Oxford University Press, 2000.

Fravel, M.T., *Strong Borders, Secure Nation: Cooperation and Conflict in China's Territorial Disputes*, Princeton: Princeton University Press, 2008.

Garver, J., *Foreign Relations of the People's Republic of China*, Englewood Cliffs, N.J.: Prentice Hall, 1993.

Goncharov, S.N., Lewis, J.W. and Xue, L., *Uncertain Partners: Stalin, Mao, and the Korean War*, Stanford: Stanford University Press, 1993.

Gries, P.H., *China's New Nationalism: Pride, Politics, and Diplomacy*, Berkeley: University of California Press, 2004.

Han, N. *et al.*, *Diplomacy of Contemporary China*, Hong Kong: New Horizon Press, 1990.

Hunt, M.H., *The Genesis of Chinese Communist Foreign Policy*, New York: Columbia University Press, 1996.

Keith, R.C., *The Diplomacy of Zhou Enlai*, London: Macmillan, 1989.

Lampton, D.M., ed., *The Making of Chinese Foreign and Security Policy in the Era of Reform*, Stanford: Stanford University Press, 2001.

Li, L., translated by Ling, Y. and Zhang, S., *Breaking Through: The Birth of China's Opening-up Policy*, New York: Oxford University Press, 2009.

Liu, X., *Chinese Ambassadors: The Rise of Diplomatic Professionalism since 1949*, Hong Kong: Hong Kong University Press, 2001.

Luthi, L.M., *The Sino-Soviet Split: Cold War in the Communist World*, Princeton: Princeton University Press, 2008.

Mitter, R., *A Bitter Revolution: China's Struggle with the Modern World*, Oxford: Oxford University Press, 2004.

Nathan, A.J. and Ross, R.S., *The Great Wall and the Empty Fortress: China's Search for Security*, New York: W. W. Norton, 1997.

Qing, S., *From Allies to Enemies: Visions of Modernity, Identity, and U.S.–China Diplomacy, 1945–1960*, Cambridge, Mass.: Harvard University Press, 2007.

Radchenko, S., *Two Suns in the Heavens: The Sino-Soviet Struggle for Supremacy, 1962–1967*, Stanford: Stanford University Press, 2009.

Richardson, S., *China, Cambodia, and the Five Principles of Peaceful Coexistence*, New York: Columbia University Press, 2010.

Roberts, P., ed., *Behind the Bamboo Curtain: China, Vietnam, and the World beyond Asia*, Stanford: Stanford University Press, 2006.

Robinson, T.W. and Shambaugh, D., eds, *Chinese Foreign Policy: Theory and Practice*, Oxford: Clarendon Press, 1995.

Sheng, M.M., *Battling Western Imperialism: Mao, Stalin, and the United States*, Princeton: Princeton University Press, 1997.

Shih, C.–Y., *China's Just World: The Morality of Chinese Foreign Policy*, Boulder: Lynne Rienner Publishers, 1993.

Scott, D., *China Stands Up: The PRC and the International System*, London: Routledge, 2007.

Wang, G., *The Chinese Way: China's Position in International Relations*, Oslo: Scandinavian University Press, 1995.

Westad, O.A., *Cold War and Revolution: Soviet–American Rivalry and the Origins of the Chinese Civil War, 1944–1946*, New York: Columbia University Press, 1993.

Westad, O.A., ed., *Brothers in Arms: The Rise and Fall of the Sino-Soviet Alliance, 1945–1963*, Stanford: Stanford University Press, 1998.

Whiting, A.S., *China Crosses the Yalu*, Stanford: Stanford University Press, 1968.

Xia, Y., *Negotiating with the Enemy: US–China Talks during the Cold War, 1949–1972*, Bloomington: Indiana University Press, 2006.

Zhai, Q., *China and the Vietnam Wars, 1950–1975*, Chapel Hill: The University of North Carolina Press, 2000.

Zhang, S.G., *Deterrence and Strategic Culture: Chinese–American Confrontations 1949–1958*, Ithaca: Cornell University Press, 1992.

Zhang, S.G., *Mao's Military Romanticism: China and the Korean War, 1950–1953*, Lawrence: University Press of Kansas, 1995.

Zhao, K.K., *Zhou Enlai and the Foundations of Chinese Foreign Policy*, New York: Macmillan, 1996.

Index